WHAT IT TAKES
TO BE FREE

WHAT IT TAKES TO BE FREE

Religion and the Roots of Democracy

Siobhan Nash-Marshall

Foreword by Dr. Seana Sugrue

A Herder & Herder Book
The Crossroad Publishing Company
New York

The Crossroad Publishing Company
www.crossoroadpublishing.com

Printed in the United States of America

This book is set in 11/14 Caslon. The display type is Caslon Antique.

Library of Congress Cataloging-in-Publication Data

Nash-Marshall, Siobhan.
    What it takes to be free : religion and the roots of democracy /
Siobhan Nash-Marshall ; foreword by Seana Sugrue.
        p.   cm.
    Includes bibliographical references.
    ISBN 0-8245-1994-9 (alk. paper)
    1. Liberty – Religious aspects. 2. Religion and politics – United
States.   I. Title.
BL65.L52N37 2003
323.44'0973 – dc21

                                            2003012513

TO THOSE WHO ARE MINE,
BORN AND UNBORN.

How few of the human race have ever had an opportunity of choosing a system of government for themselves and their children? How few have ever had anything more of choice in government than in the climate? — John Adams, letter to William Hooper

Nisi Dominus aedificaverit domum, in vanum laboraverunt qui aedificant eum. Nisi Dominus custodierit civitatem, frustra vigilat qui custodit eam.

— Psalm 126

Contents

7

Five   The Promise of Freedom   120

Foreword

Were it not for September 11, this book would not have been written. It was an event that changed the lives of Americans in profound ways. Americans have become a more introspective people; a people who ask what it means to be American, and who are, on the whole, proud of their history and the intellectual traditions that spawned the founding of their still young republic. It is this singularly important event that has led Professor Nash-Marshall, an American philosopher with a deep understanding of European cultures, to participate in a public conversation about how America ought to be understood.

This book about America, and its strengths and vulnerabilities, is quite properly a meditation on freedom. No other value is more closely associated with what it means to be American than this. From the quest of the Puritans for religious freedom to the American Revolution, from the Civil War to the war against terrorism, it is freedom that has been at stake.

When she views America from a philosophical lens or from a cosmopolitan perspective, however, Nash-Marshall perceives that freedom is not simply an American value. It is a universal good rooted in the human condition. As rational animals, we have the capacity to understand our world, to make normative judgments, and to decide how to act. A rational animal cannot do otherwise than to exercise freedom of thought, and to a more limited extent, to act freely. Hence, freedom is not simply an essential part of what it means to be American; it is part of what it means to be human.

In this book, the author weaves together the contingencies of the American experience with enduring insights about the nature of freedom. She asks who we are, and answers by looking both to American history and to a philosophical understanding of humanity. She offers glimmers of the particularity of America, while she defends a notion of freedom that transcends time and place. She portrays freedom as not simply a matter of the constitutional rights of Americans, but as a fully human right rooted in our very beings.

The deeply philosophical currents of this book explore why freedom ought to be valued, while probing the risks freedom can pose to each of us and to our communities. To the question: why value freedom? — the author offers two answers. The first and less fundamental of these is that an alternative form of government would be worse. Taking a theocracy based on divine law as the best theoretical alternative, she argues that theocracy is doomed to failure because it cannot achieve through coercive means its end of true conversion to faith. One cannot coerce thought or conscience.

However, a second and more essential response is also provided to why freedom is of value. Not only is freedom part of our nature, but like life and rationality, it is also a prerequisite to the pursuit of all human ends, including happiness and good government. An appropriate form of government must be one that is suited to our natures, and as beings who think freely, the principles that guide us must be accepted freely. Good government is one that allows for the bounties made possible by human freedom; it does not suppress freedom. Hence a government appropriate to a free people is one through which we consent to the laws that govern us.

Professor Nash-Marshall recognizes, however, that this conclusion begets a number of paradoxes. At the heart of these paradoxes is the fact that human beings do not necessarily exercise their liberty well. Not all human ends are laudable, let alone well conceived. Democracies can be oppressive, or less dramatically, their people can be apathetic. Additionally, a free people are often divided by differences of opinion.

Taking diversity of opinion, or disunity, as a principal challenge to a political community, Nash-Marshall motions once again to that which is universal — standards of judgment external to our own personal preferences. These standards are found in the external world, in our common language, in rules of logic, and in our shared humanity. In the end, it is argued that truth coupled with an ethos of personal responsibility curb the dangers inherent in being a free, self-governing people.

Historical anecdotes illustrate the philosophical argument, and do much more. They also sketch how America has become the land of the free by presenting a portrait of the striking and distinctive qualities of its people. Among these characteristics are faith in a Creator, an independent spirit, and a penchant for practicality. These qualities, not shared to the same degree by peoples of most other nations, are depicted as cultural conditions that have made America fertile soil for self government.

Hence in revisiting the question of what it takes to be free, Professor Nash-Marshall provides two provocative answers. In one sense, we simply are free by virtue of being human. But this is not what most of us understand by freedom. We want freedom *and* the bounties of other virtues and goods, including good government. To achieve this synthesis, there are no simple answers. However, Professor Nash-Marshall understands that we do well to study the American experiment with ordered liberty to begin.

SEANA SUGRUE

One

Why Freedom?

America is a wonder. There has never been a nation quite like ours, and there probably never will be another. We are the envy of the world. People have come from all corners of the globe in order to become a part of our world. They followed those metropolitan whispers that claimed that America's streets are paved in gold, that America is the land of opportunity, that America is the land of milk and honey. Those who came discovered that our streets are not paved in gold, and that milk and honey, although readily available, needed to be paid for. But still they stayed and sent for their families. And those whispers that spoke of us with awe continued to circulate abroad. Those whispers can still be heard in faraway lands if we listen carefully enough. Europeans still look with wonder upon our world. They imitate our dress. They imitate our mannerisms. They even imitate our speech. Modern Italian, German, and French are laden with American idioms. Germans have complained to me that they "earn peanuts" — "verdiene Peanuts" — and that that is not "cool" — "nicht cool." Frenchmen have told me over cocktails that their "jobs" — "mon job" — make them work on the "weekend" — "le weekend," which should perhaps be spelled "ouiquende" in their case. Besides using a formidable array of American idioms that range from "drink" to "soft,"

Italians even invent their own American-sounding idioms to make their products sound more attractive. I was offered a "shopper" for my purchases at the checkout counter in a store in Venice. "Uno shopper," the kind clerk told me when she saw that I looked puzzled, is a shopping bag. These foreign whispers concerning us have turned harsh in some lands. Our country is truly hated in parts of the world today. We had tangible proof of this on September 11. But even that hatred is a tribute to the wonder that is our country. For as much as it may be caused by some of our mistakes, that hatred would not be as intense as it is if we were not the miracle we are. It takes more than journalists, governments, and our mistakes to cause the intense hatred of our country that so many people feel abroad. It takes envy, fear, and awe. These are the feelings that our nation inspires abroad. We are a wonder to the entire world.

There is something poetic about our being the envy of the world. Our ancestors were certainly not the envy of the world when they came to our country. They would probably not have braved the elements if they had been. Coming to America was often a dangerous and difficult thing to do. And people do not tend to do dangerous and difficult things just for the fun of it. Our ancestors came to this country in search of a future. They came because they had no real future in the lands from which they escaped. Our ancestors came because they were the forgotten, the downtrodden, in their worlds. They were the poor, the misunderstood, the futureless who yearned for prosperity, understanding, and futures. The children of those ancestors have risen to become citizens of the most powerful, vibrant, successful, generous, and envied nation in the world, calling to mind that wonderful doctrine that "the last will come first."

What makes us different? What is the secret of the American wonder? The root of the answer primarily has to do with freedom, with our love and understanding of freedom. Our nation was founded on the quest for freedom. Every important event in our history had the quest for freedom as its primary cause. The Pilgrims came to this country because they sought religious freedom. The Founding Fathers of our country declared our independence in the name of freedom. We even fought the Civil War in the name of freedom. The North fought to bring freedom to the slaves. The South fought to defend its freedom to live as it saw fit. Freedom is our air, our water, our battle cry.

But what is freedom, why is it so important to us, and above all what does it really take for a people be the land of the free? I cannot possibly answer all of these questions in this book. Freedom is a fundamental reality whose ramifications are so widespread that one cannot but give the topic short shrift in a book, especially if that book is short. Freedom is one of the defining characteristics of human beings. It touches on nearly every aspect of human life, from the religious to the civil, from the public to the private. This is, for instance, why it plays a significant role in the debate between evolutionists and creationists. If we are free, creationists claim, then we cannot really explain all of human behavior in biological terms. Freedom is not a biological fact. But if we cannot explain all of human behavior in biological terms, then we cannot expect biology to give us a complete picture of human life or of the guiding principles of human nature. Thus, creationists claim, to teach evolutionism to the exclusion of creationism is a grave mistake. It is to overlook one of the crucial aspects of being human. Human freedom is also a fundamental presupposition of our justice system. It would make no sense to punish or praise people for their behavior if people were not responsible for their behavior. And people could not be responsible for their behavior if they were not free to choose how to act. Justice would be an empty word if there were no such thing as freedom. Freedom plays a significant role in the religious picture. Adam and Eve could eat the apple because they were free. But explaining just how human beings can be free if God knows all of their acts from eternity is no mean feat. Philosophers and theologians have been debating this matter for millennia. Freedom plays an important part in our thoughts. There is an important sense in which we could not think if we were not free. Freedom plays an enormous role in our personal relations. How often do we fear commitment because we are afraid that it will stifle our freedom? The point is that there is hardly an aspect of human life in which freedom does not play some role. Thus, to talk about freedom, human freedom, is in some basic sense to talk about everything it is to be human. It is not by chance that our Founding Fathers claimed that all inalienable human rights, and not just the right to liberty, are essential to building the land of the free. To build the land of the free is in a crucial sense to build the land that protects everything it is to be human. But as this is so, to explain what freedom is and why it is so important to us entails explaining everything it means to be human, from human ontology to human psychology, from justice to religion, from human acts to human interrelations. Freedom is not just any word or fact. It is a basic one. Dealing with basic facts takes more than just a short book.

My intent in this book is something else. It is to spell out the conditions that make it possible for a nation to be the land of the free, what it takes for us to be the land of the free. It is to look at the problems that those who would build and inhabit the land of the free must face and solve. It is to look at ourselves and our history to understand what we can never forsake if we are to be true to ourselves and our quest for freedom.

Why We Need to Understand Freedom

There has never been a time when it was more important or urgent for us to understand what it takes to be free. We are being attacked because we love freedom, because we believe that human beings have *inalienable* rights, and because our love and beliefs have made us the most vibrant, successful, generous, and envied nation in the world. What we have to do in order to really win this war is to understand just what it means to love freedom, what we mean when we say that human beings have inalienable rights, and why no nation should not protect freedom and the other inalienable rights that we all have. There is only one way to win an ideological war — which is the kind of war in which we are embroiled — and that is to understand the principles that have come under attack, to demonstrate that they are not simply *alternative* principles, principles among many that have the equal right to be called great, but are *superior* principles, and to live in accordance with them.

It is also important and urgent for us to understand what it takes to be free, independently of this war. We are in many ways a nation that is "searching for a public philosophy,"[1] a cogent and coherent way of putting together our public needs and private rights, our national and international interests and responsibilities. Ours is not a winter of discontent. It is a time of real search. We are in some sense like that people described in the Psalms, the generation who is waiting for the voice from above that will explain what is to be done and how it is to be done. We are anxious. We squabble among ourselves precisely because we are anxious.

Our anxiety and our search have many causes. The century that came to a close threw a series of new problems and new roles on and at our nation. We are newly emerged as the world's one superpower, with all of the problems and responsibilities that this entails. We have also discovered that our own past is not as spotless as we wanted, and we are trying to come to terms with this fact. Both of these things — our new international role and our new perception of our past — have to some degree altered our perception of ourselves and our goals. Things that seemed so simple for our parents and grandparents — like knowing who the bad guys and good guys are, knowing how to put together our individual needs and the needs of our families, our neighbors, and our country, knowing how to define our values in relation to the values of others — do not seem quite as simple for us.

Our international role and internal problems were not entirely unexpected. Many of our Founding Fathers were convinced that our country would become the greatest power in the world. John Adams, for instance, predicted that the

United States would "form the greatest empire in the world." He claimed as much in a letter to Nathan Webb when he was all of 19.[2] Many of the Founding Fathers were also aware of the skeletons that were creeping into the closets of our fledgling nation as it was being founded. Slavery was one of these skeletons. John Adams's wife, Abigail, wrote as much in a letter to her husband while the First Continental Congress was taking place. "I wish most sincerely," she claimed, "that there was not a slave in the province. It always seemed a most iniquitous scheme to me — [to] fight ourselves for what we are daily robbing and plundering from those who have as good a right to freedom as we have."[3] The Founding Fathers also knew that these skeletons would return to haunt us. There were many reasons for their concern. Slavery was the most divisive topic in the Union, and the Founding Fathers realized that if no cure could be found for the division it caused, it might lead to a serious conflict.[4] What were more important than the national divisions, at least from our perspective, were the consequences of slavery: the prejudice, anger, and guilt that it would leave in its wake. Some of the Founding Fathers thought that these consequences made eradicating the effects of slavery impossible if the emancipated slaves continued to live in our nation. Thomas Jefferson's *Notes on the State of Virginia* make this point very clearly. "Deep rooted prejudices entertained by the whites — ten thousand recollections by the blacks of the injuries they have sustained — new provocations . . . and many other circumstances which divide us into parties, and produce convulsions which would never end but with the extermination of one or the other race."[5] Jefferson's view on this matter was, of course, extreme. But it was accurate in one respect at least. Slavery did not become a dead issue once Lincoln issued the Emancipation Proclamation. Its effects, like the effects of those other skeletons that our closets hid, are to some degree with us still.

But as expected as our internal problems and our massive international role were, no one expected them to drop like bombshells upon our shoulders quite as suddenly as they did, or at the same time. But this is in some sense precisely what happened. At the beginning of the twentieth century, there were many world powers: England, France, Germany, Austria, Italy, and even Belgium and Holland. By the mid 1950s these many powers had been replaced by two: our nation and Russia. By 1990 we stood alone as the world's one superpower. This was all quick, very quick. It was quick in historical terms, just as is everything about our nation. Our nation grew at lightning speed. It was also very quick for our nation. Fifty years are not much time for any people to become accustomed to being a superpower, especially a people like ours who had a primarily isolationist mentality during the first century of its existence.[6]

It did not take long for the breathtaking speed with which the international change of guard took place to produce its effects within our nation. Some ten years after our emergence as a superpower, a good many people in our nation began to question our international role. Many were uneasy with it, and for a multitude of reasons. To some, our being a superpower seemed to be contrary to our principles. John Adams may not have had any qualms about using the word "empire" when describing his hopes for our nation, but by the latter half of the twentieth-century many Americans did. The

cause of their reticence was not just the brutality of twentieth century empires. There was a more basic issue involved
in American horror of empires. Freedom and empires are not
good bedfellows. Empires are formed when one nation imposes its way of life, its will, upon others, and imposition
seems to be the farthest thing from freedom. If it is freedom we are after, many claimed, empires cannot be a viable
part of our plan. To form an empire is to give up on our
quest for freedom.[7] But our being a superpower seemed to
imply that we are an empire or that we could become one.
Thus, many objected in principle to our power and international role. Our international role also seemed to give our
national affairs secondary status. Maintaining a large stand-
ing army absorbs a lot of money and resources which, some
argued, could be better spent. Why should we worry about
other nations and peoples, it was asked, if we have plenty of
problems of our own that we cannot deal with if we spend
too much time looking abroad? Above all, our international
role was new, and we, the people of the United States, did
not quite know how to deal with it. It constituted a major
change for us, and change is not always easy. Our reaction
to our emergence as a superpower is, I am sure, no different
from those of many of the superpowers of the past. If we
were to leaf through the initial reactions of private Romans
to the growing international role and presence of their republic, we would undoubtedly find that many of them were
uneasy with it too. Many of them certainly thought that it
was contrary to the principles of the Roman republic. Many
of them certainly thought that if Rome focused too much
of its attention abroad, the republic would suffer. Of course,

many of them were proud of their new power, and some took advantage of it. But on the whole Roman reactions to their growth of power must have been mixed; that power must have many Romans uneasy.

As for those internal problems that we came to be aware of in the latter half of the twentieth century, they were in some sense triggered by our uneasiness with our international role. To be sure, these problems were lying under the surface of our country's daily affairs, ready to jump out at us at any time. Skeletons hidden in closets are like that. But questioning our international role, which was prompted by our emergence as one of the world's two superpowers, was a quick route to a more general questioning of ourselves, our past, and our principles, which our country began to experience on a large scale some thirty years ago. To some, our fighting abroad felt very much like those skeletons hidden in our closets and were the demonstration that our principles were not sound, or that we did not adhere to them.

The changes in our perception of ourselves have left us somewhat breathless. We are to some degree still unsure of ourselves and our future. This is not to say that it was not necessary for us to come to terms with our past or with those effects of our past that are still lingering in the present. Nor is it to say that it is not right to question our international role. If there is any sign of the greatness of our nation, of our great vitality and potential, and of our general moral health, it is precisely the fact that we can and do question ourselves. That we can and do want to correct our past mistakes and keep from making further ones. It is to say that all of the questioning has left us searching for a "public philosophy," a coherent and cogent expression of our principles, a coherent and cogent way of putting together our public needs and private rights, our national and international responsibilities and interests. By questioning our past, we also questioned what we are and what we should be. We discarded those stock formulas with which our parents and grandparents defined being American. The problem is that discarding old formulas does not necessarily yield new formulas. And in our case it has not yet. Not enough time has passed for us to have come up with a new resounding understanding of what it means to be American. It is precisely times like these that call for us to get back to the basics and take a good look at the guiding principles of our nation.

The Conditions of Freedom

There are many ways of examining a nation's principles. One can do so historically, by analyzing how and why those principles emerged, how they were understood when they did emerge, and how this understanding has changed through time. One can do so legally, by analyzing a nation's principles in terms of their constitutional meaning. One can do so sociologically, by analyzing the meaning of a nation's principles in terms of their immediate and long-term effects on people and societies. This book analyzes our principles philosophically. Its intention is to delineate the conditions of building the land of the free, to explain the importance of these minimum requisites of building the land of the free, and to examine the ground of these conditions, what makes them sound. The intention is, in other words, to go back to the drawing board and ask why we want to be the land of the free, what rules the land of the free must have, why we should accept and respect those rules, and how we can accept and respect those rules without losing our freedom.

From the philosophical point of view, there are two basic conditions to building the land of the free. The first is that those who would build and inhabit the land of the free must be convinced that freedom is the primary value, something of intrinsic worth that should be loved and pursued over and above other values, other things of intrinsic worth. The second is that freedom must be pursuable not just by individuals singly, but by a nation as a whole, the battle cry not just of single people who want individually to affirm their rights, but of a nation as a whole.

Both of these conditions are problematic. The first condition naturally calls anyone who would build or inhabit the land of the free to explain why freedom — rather than a host of other things of intrinsic worth — should be considered a land's or people's primary value. This is not as easy as it sounds. Freedom is an important human characteristic. But it is not the only important human characteristic and, what is more important, it has presuppositions. We could not be free if we did not exist. Nor could we be free if we were not rational. To defend the claim that freedom is a primary value, as such, entails explaining not only why freedom is the primary value, but also how it can be a primary value, when it would not seem logical for it to be one, precisely because it has presuppositions. That is, to claim that freedom is what matters most is to claim that it is a more important value than life or than rationality. But freedom, it would seem, cannot be a more important value than life or rationality. We cannot be free if we do not live or are not rational. Thus, even if freedom is an important thing, it would seem difficult to claim that it is more important than life or rationality. So why exactly do we think that freedom is the primary value? How can we claim that it is our most important value? And what exactly do we mean when we do claim that it is our most important value?

The second condition is even more complex. Freedom seems only to belong to single people. The Declaration of Independence claims that it is "self-evident" that liberty is the inalienable right of "all men." It does not claim that it belongs to nations. Herein lies the problem. Human beings are not nations. They are individuals. And individuals and nations have different needs and requirements. Nations require laws. Nations require consent. But requirements in themselves seem to limit freedom. So too do the specific requirements of building a nation — laws and consent — seem to limit freedom. Thus, the rights of individuals and the needs and requirements of nations seem to be at odds with each other. This seems to make building or inhabiting the land of the free an impossible task. If the right of individual human beings to freedom must take precedence over the rights of nations — since it is freedom that our nation is built on, and freedom only belongs to individual human beings, in this world at least — then it would seem necessary to claim that no nation can limit human beings' freedom in any way. But this would imply that there can be no such thing as a nation built on freedom. Building or inhabiting a nation seems necessarily to limit human beings' freedom. Nations require laws. They require consent. So it would seem impossible to build a nation on freedom.

The point is that from the philosophical point of view, building the land of the free involves two basic paradoxes. The first is the paradox involved in claiming that freedom is a primary value. The second is the paradox involved in building a nation on freedom. The success of one's building the land of the free depends upon the success with which he solves these paradoxes.

Our Love of Freedom

We take it for granted that freedom is the central human value. This is not just because we believe that this truth is self-evident, that all persons have "the inalienable right to liberty." The Declaration of Independence also claims that men have the inalienable right to "life, and the pursuit of happiness," but we do not put the premium on the right to life, equality, or the pursuit of happiness. We put the premium on freedom. We call ourselves the "land of the free," not the "land of those who pursue happiness," the "land of the equal," or the "land of those who live," even though the Declaration of Independence claims that we are "created equal" and that we have the "inalienable right to life" before it claims that we have the inalienable right to freedom. Why do we value freedom as much as we do? This is the first crucial question when it comes to our country. It may be a self-evident truth that human beings are free, but it is not a self-evident truth that freedom has to take first place among all of the things to which we have an inalienable right.

To put the point another way, there are several distinctive human characteristics. Freedom is one of them. It is not the only one. Rationality is another. The capacity to love is yet another. There are also many important human virtues: honor, loyalty, courage, generosity, magnanimity, honesty, humility, truthfulness. All of these characteristics are fundamental to nation building. Rationality is essential to nations. Without it people could not formulate laws or understand laws, and laws are a prerequisite of any nation. The capacity to love also seems essential to nations. Nations are large communities, and communities require some kind of emotional bond between people, or else people would constantly be at each other's throats. But love is just that sort of bond. So all those who would build nations must presuppose that all those who would inhabit that nation be rational and capable of love, that is, if they want to build a just nation. Honor, loyalty, generosity, magnanimity, honesty, humility, and truthfulness seem to be essential to communities. All of these virtues have to do either directly or indirectly with people's relations to one another. This is obviously true of virtues like loyalty and generosity. But it is also true of virtues like honor and humility. Humility is a condition of accepting other people's opinions and beliefs. Honor is a condition of abiding by common principles like respect for others. And both accepting others' beliefs and respecting them have everything to do with people's relations with each other. But that which has to do with people's relations with each other has to do with nations. Nations are collections of relations. Thus, a people who want to build a prosperous and just land must presuppose that all those who would inhabit their nation have these virtues. So if all of these characteristics and virtues are essential to nations, why does freedom take precedence for us? Why not rationality? Why not honor, loyalty, or some other important virtue? Why are we the "land of the free" and not "the land of the thinkers" or the "land of the loyal"?

Nor is freedom just one among many of those human characteristics and virtues that all nations require. Freedom presupposes some of those virtues and characteristics. We cannot be free if we do not exist. Life is a prerequisite of freedom. This, presumably, is why the Founding Fathers claimed that all men have the inalienable right to life before they claimed that all men have the inalienable right to liberty. "We hold these truths to be self-evident, that all men are created equal, and endowed by their Creator with certain inalienable rights, which include *life*, liberty, and the pursuit of happiness." But if freedom presupposes life, how can freedom be the central human value for us? Should life not be more important to us than freedom, since we cannot be free if we do not live? "Give me liberty, or give me death" is a fine statement, but one must be alive in order to make it. What do we mean when we claim that freedom is the central human value? Is there not something absurd about this claim?

The answer to these questions has to do with a truth that our ancestors discovered through their own experience. Freedom is in some sense a presupposition of all true virtues. We cannot be honorable if we do not choose to be bound by our honor. The same thing holds for loyalty, courage, generosity, magnanimity, and the other human virtues. We cannot really be loyal, brave, generous, or any other good thing if we do not choose to be. Thus, if virtues are essential to nations, freedom must be too. Freedom is a presupposition of all true virtues. But virtues *are* important to nations. Nations cannot prosper if people are not virtuous — if they are not loyal, brave, or honest. If one really wants to build a strong and prosperous nation, as such, then one must allow everyone to choose to be virtuous. One must build the land on freedom. Forsaking freedom in this case is to forsake the truth in an important sense. To impose loyalty, courage, or any other virtue on people — not to allow people to choose to be loyal or brave — is to produce false loyalty, courage, or any other virtue. If true virtues are a prerequisite of a strong and healthy nation, a nation that imposes virtues on a people cannot be a strong and healthy nation. The same thing can be said for rationality and love. Human beings must also be free if they are to develop their rationality fully and if they are to love truly. We cannot really force anyone to think any more than we can force anyone to love. If rationality and love are presuppositions of strong and healthy nations, as such, freedom must be too, and in some sense more than that very rationality and love.

The point here is that although freedom has presuppositions — that beings who are capable of being free exist — it is in turn the presupposition of any free being's development and living in a community. Freedom is one of the presuppositions of all true human development and cohabitation. This is why freedom is so important to us. Freedom is the necessary requisite of human happiness and nations. This point comes with a twist. If we cherish freedom because it is a requisite of true human development and human communities, then there must be a sense in which we cannot consider freedom our primary value at all. If we cherish freedom for the sake of true human development, then we must cherish human development more than we do freedom. Human life and happiness must be more important to us than human freedom alone, if we love freedom because we want human beings to be everything that they can be. Thus when we claim that freedom is our primary value, we mean it in a specific sense. Freedom is our primary value because it is the condition of other values that are even more important to us than freedom is, values that could not be attained without freedom. Freedom is our primary value because it is the indispensable means of human happiness.

This point is important. It is what allows us to solve the paradox inherent in claiming that freedom is our primary value when there is a significant case in which it cannot be, since freedom has presuppositions. For in believing that freedom is our primary value because it is the requisite of other values, we avoid falling in the trap that would make it impossible for us to claim that freedom is a primary value. We avoid the contradiction inherent in claiming that freedom is a primary value. That is, if we were to take freedom to be our primary value in an absolute sense, we would have to believe that freedom has value independently of all other values. But we cannot possibly believe that freedom has value independently of all other values. In order for freedom to have value independently of all other values, freedom would have not to presuppose other values, things with value. Freedom does, however, presuppose other values, things with value. It presupposes life and rationality, and both of these things have value. Freedom is a *being's* characteristic. What this means is that freedom cannot be a primary value in an absolute sense. Freedom is not and cannot be an absolute value. If we were to claim that freedom is our primary value because it is an absolute value, we could not make a valid claim, and there would be no justification for building the land of the free. But this is not what we claim. Our Declaration of Independence, if not our own rationality, does not allow us to claim it.

Freedom and Nations

The second paradox involved in building the land of the free has to do with the relation between freedom and nations. At first sight, freedom and nations seem to be an uneasy mix. We feel the uneasiness of this mix every time we have to pay taxes, a parking ticket, or go on jury duty. Nations put serious limits on freedom. There are many reasons for this. The most obvious is that nations require laws, and laws seem to limit our freedom. Laws impose behavior, and impositions impede freedom. The deepest reason has to do with the very notion of government. If a people is to be a nation, they need government. But governments necessarily limit citizens' rights. The Founding Fathers were very aware of this: "Nothing is more certain than the indispensable necessity of government; and it is equally undeniable that whenever and however it is instituted, the people must cede to it some of their natural rights, in order to vest it with requisite powers."[8] As this is so, it seems contradictory to claim that a nation can be built on freedom. How can a nation be built on that which it necessarily limits?

Our ancestors had an ingenious solution to this paradox: democracy. Their insight was simple. Laws and ceding any degree of one's rights to a government can contradict freedom and human beings' other rights only if people do not freely consent to laws or to cede a part of their rights to their government. For the moment that people do freely consent to laws, or to cede a portion of their rights to their government, laws cannot limit their freedom any more than freely ceding rights can. Free acts do not limit freedom. If I freely agree to follow the head of my department's orders and to fulfill those obligations assigned to me, I cannot relinquish my freedom by following that person's orders. What this means, of course, is that a people who do freely consent to their government, and who freely accept the laws of its government, can be a nation based on freedom. It can be the land of the free. This is why the Declaration of Independence can claim that the purpose of governments is "to secure these [inalienable] rights" without being contradictory. It presupposes that "just governments derive their power from the consent of the governed." Consent preserves freedom. One can build the land of the free if one builds it on free consent.

As obvious as this solution is to the paradox of freedom and nations, however, it is a problematic solution. For as true as it is that nations built on freedom must be built on the consent of the governed, consent alone does not guarantee that a nation will be the land of the free. It is more than just theoretically possible for an entire people — or for a majority thereof — to consent freely to unjust laws, laws that negate the inalienable rights of others to freedom. It is also more than just theoretically possible for an entire people — or for a majority thereof — to cede freely a portion of their rights to a government that passes unjust laws. Things like this have happened, and not just in foreign nations. Our own government, which stood in place through the free consent of the people, did pass some unjust laws — laws that negated the inalienable rights of others — to which many people freely consented. Slavery was legal for some ninety years in our nation. Women did not have the right to vote for over a century of our nation's history. So what is to keep a people from making similar mistakes? The clear answer to this question is that there must be some standard to which the consent of the governed must conform. There must be some things that cannot be acceptable in the land of the free even if the majority of those who would live in the land of the free freely consent to them.

The problem with this answer is that it points to a paradox of its own. It would not seem possible for a people really to be the land of the free if some things there are off limits to them. Thus, if building the land of the free necessarily implies that some things must be unacceptable, even if they are things to which people can freely consent, the land of the free, it would seem, cannot be the land of the free. This is the deepest paradox of our nation. It would seem to imply that the land of the free does not have freedom alone as its foundation. If some things — actions, thoughts, or any other such thing — are unacceptable, even if they can be freely chosen, then freedom cannot be the one criterion that determines a thing's — action, thought, or any other such thing — acceptability, and consequently the land of the free cannot, it would seem, be built upon freedom.

This paradox too has a solution, which is obvious if we look closely at what we mean when we claim that freedom is our primary value. In order to claim that a nation that is not grounded exclusively on freedom cannot be the land of the free, one must believe that freedom has no presuppositions of its own. That we protect freedom for no other reason than to protect freedom. That freedom is our primary value because it is self-justifying. That it is our primary value because it is an absolute value. For the moment that we protect freedom in order to protect values other than freedom, it is obvious that the land of the free cannot be exclusively grounded in freedom. It must also be grounded in those values that we protect by protecting freedom. The moment that freedom has presuppositions of its own, then the land of the free cannot be grounded exclusively in freedom. It must also be grounded in those values that freedom presupposes. But freedom cannot be an absolute value, and it is not an absolute value for us. Freedom presupposes other things of value: the value of human life and rationality. And we protect freedom because it is the indispensable means of human happiness. What this means is that the land of the free must also be grounded in the value of human life, rationality, and the belief that human happiness cannot be forsaken. Indeed, it means that human life, our rationality, our happiness, rather than freedom alone, must be the ultimate criteria of the acceptable and the non-acceptable in the land of the free. To be built on freedom is to be built upon certain self-evident truths, truths to which all thinkers must consent. To be built on freedom is to be built on the inviolability of human life and the human search for happiness. "We hold these truths to be self-evident, that all men are created equal, and endowed by the Creator with certain inalienable rights, which include life, liberty, and the pursuit of happiness."

What It Takes to Be Free

This book is about the conditions that make it possible for a nation to be the land of the free. It is about those paradoxes that we, our ancestors, and our Founding Fathers had to solve in order to become the land of the free. These paradoxes are interrelated, and every generation must understand them, come to terms with them, grasp how they are interrelated, and map out a coherent way of solving them. Being the land of the free is not a one-time deal. It is not a math problem that can be solved once and for all generations. It is a constant challenge. This does not make it any less worthwhile for us to solve our paradoxes, or to live up to the challenge. We are not the envy of the world by chance. Our dream, the American Dream, is a beautiful one.

Two

Why We Are Not a Theocracy

The Root of Our Love of Freedom

There is something jarring about the mentality of Islamic fundamentalists — that mentality that would have religious dogma restrict human freedom and the human rights to life and the pursuit of happiness, which would condone such things as *jihad,* holy war, or "the expansion of Islam by force, if necessary,"[9] and make religious conversion from Islam to another religion a crime punishable by death.[10] There is something jarring about a mentality that would make a religious law, the *Shari'a,* a nation's civil law.

I may feel as strongly as I do about this matter because I belong to the female half of the human race, and I am horrified by the very thought of having to clamp my mind and hide my face, which is what I would have to do if I were to live under Islamic fundamentalist rule. Women were punished in Afghanistan for doing such innocent things as teaching girls how to write and not wearing a *burkha,* a veil that completely covered their faces. Although the male segment of the human population would not have to cover its face if we were to live under Islamic fundamentalist rule, it would still have to clamp its mind. Openness to thought other than Islamic fundamentalist thought can be a capital crime in Islamic fundamentalist society. The male segment of the population would also have to fear for its well-being. The draconian laws of the strictest

Islamic fundamentalist societies allow for torture. They admit confessions given under torture as evidence in their courts. They apply the eye-for-an-eye reading of the law so literally that punishments for crimes can include things like the loss of a hand or a foot. So I suppose that we should all feel jarred by the mentality of Islamic fundamentalists.

We are accustomed not only to thinking of civil law and religious law as distinct things, but also to thinking of civil laws and human rights as things that can restrict religious claims and practices. It is not illegal in our country to skip services (of whatever sort) on Sunday, although every Christian knows that it is his or her religious obligation to attend them, and the great majority of us are Christian. What is illegal in our country is to make a law that would make it illegal to skip services on Sunday, even though it is a dictate of religious law to respect the Sabbath. The first amendment to our Constitution states this clearly: "Congress shall make no law respecting an establishment of religion, or prohibiting the free exercise thereof."

We also give human rights the power to restrict religious claims and practices. Federal laws forbid polygamy, despite the fact that the Mormon religion, among others, allows for it, precisely because polygamy is a violation of human rights. Polygamy presupposes that men and women are inherently unequal. It allows one man to marry many women, but it does not allow one woman to marry many men. And this is the sort of thing that we cannot as a nation accept. Utah was not given statehood until it made polygamy illegal. Actually, it is because of the importance we accord human rights that we separate the powers of church and state. The foundation of the law of our nation is the inalienable rights of human beings. The Declaration of Independence, the Preamble of the Constitution, and the Bill of Rights all make this point clearly.

Our nation's perspective seems to be the exact opposite of that of Islamic fundamentalists. They take religious claims and law to be the unchallengeable foundation of the proper way of life and give religious claims legal precedence over human rights. Our nation takes the inalienable rights of human beings to be the unchallengeable foundation of a proper way of life, and gives these rights legal precedence over religious laws and practices. Granted, then, that our perspective is at radical odds with the Islamic perspective, on what grounds can we claim that ours is the proper perspective? Why are we not a theocracy? Or, to put the question another way, why is freedom so important to us? This is the crucial question when it comes to understanding who we are.

God's Rights and Human Rights

An atheist might claim that ours is the proper perspective because religious dictates are empty. To make religious laws the laws of a nation and to give religious laws precedence over human rights is, the atheist might claim, to do the most absurd thing possible: it is to make human life subordinate to the dictates of what does not exist. Nietzsche might have claimed this sort of thing, and there are quite a few people in our country today who take what he said very seriously. This sort of objection, however, has no validity unless one is an atheist, and most of us are not atheists.

So barring this way out of the problem, since it is one that most of us would not want to take anyway, the question should really be this: What is wrong with making religious law a nation's civil law and human rights subordinate to religious claims, if God does exist?

From a religious perspective, it would seem, there is nothing wrong with it at all. After all, if God is the sovereign of the universe, the Creator of the universe, then God's law must be absolute law. Any nation should want its law to conform as closely as possible to the highest law. If we have to have laws, they might as well be the best possible ones. What this means, of course, is that every nation should want its law to conform as closely as possible to God's law. And what way of conforming more closely to God's law is there than making it the law of one's nation? Shouldn't God's law, then, be our nation's law?

To put the point slightly differently, religion deals with what is most important to each and every one of us: our ultimate damnation or salvation, the ultimate meaning of our lives. And religious laws are designed to ensure our salvation, insofar as this is possible. Does it not make sense, then, to make those laws that deal with what is most important to us all, with the ultimate meaning of our life, with our salvation, the laws of our nation? It would certainly seem so.

As for human rights, they are, of course, important. No one would deny that. Their importance, however, seems to dwindle once one views human rights in an absolute perspective, once one puts God in the picture. After all, as much respect as human beings deserve, they must surely deserve less respect than God. God is omniscient; we are not. God's goodness is infinite; ours is not. God is omnipotent; we are

39

not. But a being's rights derive from its intrinsic worth; from the fact that its very existence warrants respect. Is this not why we would chop down trees to heat our homes, or to print our books, but would never hurt a human being to better ourselves? Is it not why we claim that human beings have inalienable rights, while trees do not?

But if a being's rights do derive from its intrinsic worth, then since God is a more significant being than we are — God has infinite wisdom and power, and we do not — it follows that God must warrant more respect than we do. What this means, of course, is that God's rights are more important than our rights. Is this not the whole point of the Book of Job? When Job called upon God to explain why God had mistreated him — Job was concerned with his rights — God responded by asking Job where he was when God laid the foundations of the universe. The point, of course, is that since God gave us everything we have, we have no right at all to question God about anything. The point is that God's rights are more important than our own.

God's rights are expressed in divine law. And what this means is that since God's rights are more important than our own, then divine law must be more important than our own laws and more important than human rights.

This is why there are such things as missionaries who are willing to die — to forsake their right to life — for their faith. God's rights are simply that much more important to them than their own. But it is not just missionaries who show how much sense this point makes. Our own personal perspective is (or should be) much the same as theirs. As important as it is to me that other people respect me, it is (or should be) much more important to me to go to heaven. I like and respect human beings, but I would much rather hear a "well done" from God than I would from my next-door neighbor or a colleague, as much as I like my neighbors and colleagues and appreciate their respect. But we get that "well done" by following divine law: by practicing the true faith in the proper manner. What this means, of course, is that practicing the true faith in the proper manner, or following divine law, is (or should be) intrinsically more important to us than the respect of other people.

But the basic minimum respect that we (should) all have from all people is for the barebones of ourselves: for our lives, our liberty, our pursuit of happiness. That minimum respect for us is for what we call our "rights." If this is so, and if following divine law is more important than other people's respect, then God's law must be more important to us than our own rights. Granted, it is easier to say this than it is to live it most of the time, but this does not change the principle.

Here is the problem: If we agree that divine law should ideally be our nation's law and that divine law does have priority over human rights, does it not follow that we should hold that our constitutional system and way of life — which give human rights priority over religious law — are inferior to the one that Islamic fundamentalists would want to impose on us? This is not to say that we should embrace Islamic as opposed to Christian divine law as our nation's law. Christians have plenty of religious laws of their own. It is to say that theocracy, a government based on divine laws, would seem to be a more perfect form of government than a democracy, which is based on human rights.

What is wrong with theocracies? On what grounds can we defend our choice as a nation not to be a theocracy? How can we claim to have a *superior* way of life with respect to those Islamic fundamentalists who are beating at our gates, if their basic point seems to make sense?

The Hazards of Theocracies

There are several obvious problems with theocracies. The most obvious is that they tend to be brutal. We saw as much on September 11, when footage of Middle Easterners making all manner of joyful noises, because some fanatic terrorists had killed infidels in God's name, was broadcast on our networks. This violence is the natural consequence of the fact that theocracies subordinate human rights to divine law. Making human rights secondary concerns is a dangerous thing. It gives theocracies the license to do any number of violent things to people, as long as they can claim to be enforcing divine law — that is, ensuring that everyone does practice the true faith in the proper manner — through their violence.

Thus, theocracies often justify executions and forced conversions on the basis of the priority of divine law over human rights. Their arguments for doing so are not absurd. After all, the worst possible scenario for a person, from the religious perspective, is to go to hell. It would seem, however, that people go to hell if they do not practice the true faith in the proper way. If this is so, then would it not seem proper to use any means at all to keep a person from not practicing the true faith in the proper way? And if torture, murder, extortion, and all manner of brutal things can, as it seems, make people practice the true faith in the proper way, should a theocratic regime not use torture to help people convert and thus save them from suffering the pains of hell? Should that regime not execute those who would not convert even under torture, in order to keep their blasphemy from infecting others?

Arguments like these have been made in the past. A brief glance through the history of our world shows just how many often brilliant people of faith were convinced by them. I do not only mean Torquemada, the person behind the Spanish Inquisition. Cotton Mather, who was by no means a fool — he wrote 450 books and was elected a Fellow of the Royal Society, which was one of the most important scientific bodies in the world at the time — was also convinced by them. When the Salem "witch" problem broke out, Mather was called upon to help determine what should be done to solve the problem. His reasons for extorting confessions from "witches" and for executing those who would not confess were not really much different from the one above: "He believed that the trials, if pursued vigorously enough, would expose the whole machinery of witchcraft and the operations of the Devil, thereby benefiting mankind enormously."[11]

Arguments like these are also being made in the present. Islamic fundamentalists make them all the time. And if one wants to accept the premises of a theocracy — that civil law should be divine law and human rights should be subordinate to both — there is, it would seem, no way of countering them. How is one to defend human rights when they are challenged by divine laws?

This alone would seem to be grounds enough for not wanting to be a theocracy. For if the premises of a theocracy lead to and justify violence against human beings, and if this sort of violence is wrong, then the premises of a theocracy must themselves be wrong. This would seem easy enough.

But most of us do not really think that the premises of a theocracy are wrong. It does seem right to claim that God's rights are more important than our own, just as it seems right to claim that divine law is the highest law. So we seem to be caught in a catch-22. On the one hand, we want to admit that the premises of a theocracy are right — that it is right to give priority to divine law with respect to human rights and to make divine law the law of one's nation. On the other hand, we want no part of the actions that can result from giving divine law priority with respect to human rights.

One of the ways to get out of this jam is to say that those theocracies that would justify and permit torture and executions are not really based on divine laws at all. For no good law would warrant killing human beings. There is a commandment on this point. So theocracies that justify and practice things like torture and execution must be based on some misconceived version of divine laws. The solution to the problem of the excesses of theocracy, as such, would seem to be to create a theocracy that is based on that set of divine laws that does not justify torture and executions. This would satisfy all of the necessary points. It would give God priority over all things; it would make one's nation's laws the highest of laws; it would not justify the carnage that is often perpetrated in God's name. The solution, in other words, would be to be a good theocracy.

And this solution would probably help us breathe more deeply, at least for a short while. We want order. It is a deep yearning in us all.

Why a Theocracy Will Not Work

And yet, as much as a theocracy sounds like an oasis for so many of us, the truth is that it is not the way to get our innocence back. Even if we as a nation were to have a very clear idea regarding the set of divine laws to use as our nation's own set of laws — which we actually do not — we would have to face the impossible task of enforcing them. And it is enforcing them that makes the whole dream of a theocracy backfire.

There are some divine laws that seem rather simple to enforce. "Thou shalt not steal" is one of them. We are enforcing this law as it is, or at least we are trying to. The same thing can be said of "Thou shalt not kill." But how is a government to enforce the commandment "Thou shalt not covet" or the commandment "Love thy neighbor as thyself, and the Lord thy God with all of thy heart"? How can a government ensure that everyone "loves" and does not "covet"? These are the laws that we would really want enforced. It is the coveting, the envy, the ruthlessness that cut into our souls. It is because people covet their neighbors' things, because they envy their neighbors, because they do not love their neighbors, that they would steal from them, kill them, cheat them, and use them.

There are two problems inherent in enforcing these specific laws. The first is that of determining who does love and who does not covet. The second is finding measures that would ensure that everyone does love and no one covets.

How is a government to tell whether someone covets something or does not love it? Love is an easy enough thing to feign. People get away with pretending to love other people all the time. Is this not one of the reasons why so many people find it so very difficult to make friends, and to have stable marriages? We all have a very hard time recognizing true love when we see it. Is this not the point Shakespeare made in *King Lear?* Like all powerful and power-hungry individuals, Lear was convinced that love was one of those things that could be demanded of people, just as a king can demand obedience. And when the time came for him to determine how much his daughters loved him, Lear mistook the flattery of his daughters Gonereil and Regan for love, and the love of his daughter Cordelia for indifference. Gonereil and Regan knew how to flutter their lashes and tell their father what he wanted to know. Cordelia, on the other hand, was a straight shooter and did not want to demean herself or her father by fluttering her eyelashes. Lear went mad once he discovered how wrong he was.

And how about coveting? How can anyone really tell when people are coveting things? To be honest, this is no easier than understanding whether people love their neighbor. This is why *Othello*'s Iago is so frightening. Iago dressed his envy in conspiracy theories and managed to convince Othello that his wife, Desdemona, was having an affair. Any one of us could fall for this trap. Sweet-talking, quick-talking people can convince anyone of anything. So how are we really to tell whether someone covets our goods, envies us, or loves us?

The first problem with theocracy is that we are not God. If we were God, we would know people's hearts and could know whether and when their thoughts conform to God's will. If we were God, we could rule our nation in an absolutely just manner, applying God's laws as they are meant to be applied.

But we are not God. We do not have God's omniscience. We do not have God's justice, God's mercy. So we really cannot rule a nation in God's name and in a way that completely conforms to God's will, no matter what anyone says. To claim to be able to do so is basically wrong. It is actually blasphemous.

Were this not enough of a problem when it comes to ensuring that we all love our neighbor and do not covet our neighbor's things, there is a second problem: no amount of enforcement can produce love. Even if there were such things as a love test or a covet test, some complicated polygraph machine that could reveal beyond reasonable doubt whether and when a person does love something, how could anyone induce persons who do not love their neighbors, or their Lord and God, to love them? If our government were to attempt to force people not to covet and to love, would we really not covet? Would we really love? It would be really hard to do so, it seems to me. If I were forced not to covet in order to avoid severe punishments, I would most probably covet the power that those who enforce this law have. And how about forcing us to love someone? This too seems impossible, even though many people do not quite seem to understand that it is. Love is a free act of will, and free acts cannot be forced. Actually, when someone attempts to force me to love something, I most often end up loathing it. We have a mean streak in us.

This points out the most basic problem with the whole notion of a theocracy: Enforcing divine laws seems to contradict the whole point of making divine laws the laws of one's nation to begin with. We would want to make divine laws the laws of our nation in order to ensure that people respect them, that no one covets and that all people love their neighbor as themselves. But the very attempt to ensure this would surely defeat itself; it could not produce love. And thus it is that theocracies end up defeating themselves. This is the basic flaw in a theocracy's premises, the fact that it misunderstands the nature of the human person and our relation to divine laws. It misunderstands the basic point of faith. Faith is a personal relation between a believer and God; it is a divine grace, a gift given by God.

Faith and Human Inviolability

The aim of theocracy is to ensure that everyone abides by divine law, that everyone respects it and cherishes it. But as atheists point out, one cannot respect and cherish divine law without believing in God. Why would we want to bother to love our Lord and God if we did not believe in God? Why would we cherish divine law if we did not think that God exists? Why would we want to love our neighbor as ourselves if we thought that the only reality is material and that human beings are just masses of cells with no intrinsic value, a superior species whose sole goal is survival? It is knowledge of God's existence that makes people respect divine law, and faith that makes one cherish it. Without knowledge and faith, a theocracy is impossible. And theocracies cannot produce faith any more than they can impose rational acceptance of God's existence on people.

Faith is much more than the mouthing of the words "God exists" or "God is great," as important as these words may be. It is more than accepting intellectually that it is plausible that God exists or accepting that God's existence is rationally demonstrable, as important as each of these things is. It is more than attending religious services, as important as this is. If it were any of these things, a government might have a hand in giving people faith.

Faith is a personal relation between a believer and God; it is a divine grace, a divine gift, which a person must freely accept. It is a conversation between a believer and God. Like all meaningful conversations, it changes the conversers. It makes them see their life and the world with and through the eyes of the person with whom they are conversing, to some degree. And this gives the conversers a new understanding of their life and the world that surrounds them. It makes them see themselves and the world with startling novelty. This is the joy of conversations in general.

This joy is incommensurately great in a conversation with God, however dim God's voice may be. Faith changes one's view on everything. Seeing things albeit "through a glass in a dark manner" through God's view, is not only to begin to see them for what they were meant to be, to begin to see their place in the order of God's universe, it is also to see them as signs of their infinitely close and distant Creator. It is to see "fire not merely as fire — a chemical reaction — but as representing the sublimity of God, and as being directed to him."[12] Through faith "the invisible things of God are clearly seen, being understood by the things that are made: His eternal power also and divinity" (Rom. 1:20). To have faith is to walk the road to Emmaus and to begin to understand what things really mean.

Like all true conversations, the conversation between God and a believer is a personal thing, and must be freely entered into. Conversations need receptive audiences, and people are only truly intellectually receptive when they freely open their minds. We can no more force people to open their minds to God freely, to accept a gift from God, whether this be by imposing formal observance of religious laws upon them person or by torturing them, than we can force God to give a gift. Actually, to try to force people to freely open their minds often has the opposite effect.

This is one of the reasons why torturing people in God's name and imposing God's law upon people in God's name is such a horrifying thing. If faith, like love, must be accepted freely, then to use torture of any sort to propagate faith is to mock faith in the same way that rape mocks love. It is to ridicule faith.

It is also to scorn God and God's creation. If human beings are capable of faith, it is because God created them so they might have personal relations with God. We were created in God's *image and likeness.* This is why faith is so important to begin with. It is the first step toward the whole point of human life. Beings who are created in the image and likeness of God must be sacred, and what is sacred must also be inviolable. To be on a first-name basis with God is no little matter. But if human beings are inviolable, then to attempt to force them to live the true faith in the proper way, by torturing them or by imposing religious laws on them, is to violate the very thing that one would want to uphold by torturing them: God's will. It is through God's will that we are inviolable. It is through God's will that our personal relations with God are to be freely entered into. It is God who gave us free will — the choice to accept God or deny God.

Faith and Freedom

It took us years and years to understand this. The Pilgrims came to our land precisely because the British Crown tried to impose a state religion upon them. The Crown of England had passed from being Catholic — Henry VIII received the title "Defender of the Faith," which the English monarch bears to this day, from Pope Leo X for having assiduously defended Catholicism against Martin Luther — to becoming Anglican, back to being Catholic, only to return to being Anglican, in the space of fewer than thirty years. And every time the Crown shifted in its religious allegiances, the people were expected (and made) to follow. To not do so was punishable by death. Thus, in 1533, after having been Catholic for nearly a millennium, the English people were expected to gleefully (and under the pain of death) acknowledge that King Henry (and not the bishop of Rome) was the rightful leader of the Church of England, simply because Henry had fought with Rome. Not doing so, as Thomas More's case illustrates, was punishable by death. In 1553, after having been Anglican for twenty years, the people were expected to return to being Catholic. In 1558, five years after the return of Catholicism as England's official religion, they were expected to become Anglicans again. This was too much for anyone. The Pilgrims and Puritans fled England to escape a system that thought that faith could be imposed upon people.

The first lesson they seemed to have learned from their experience, however, was not so much that imposing faith was wrong, but that imposing the *wrong* faith was wrong.

The Puritans did quite a bit of religious imposing of their own. They had stocks and scarlet letters for anyone who did not "love his neighbor as himself," "love his Lord and God with all of his heart," or obey the Ten Commandments. They were more than willing to jail and exile heretics, and to torture those who would not confess to witchcraft. Hawthorne has not let us forget this. When the Anabaptists pled for tolerance by appealing to the tolerance of the early settlers of Massachusetts, Increase Mather (Cotton Mather's father) responded by saying that the Anabaptists were simply mistaken with respect to the tolerance of the early settlers, since they were "professed enemies of it, and could leave the world professing that they *died no Libertines.* Their business was to settle and (as much as in them lay) to secure Religion to Posterity, according to the way which they believed was of God."[13]

Nor were the Puritans content with imposing their religious views just on the settlers of Massachusetts. During the English Civil War (1642–44), the Puritans, who had in the meanwhile gained control of England's government, made their way over to Maryland, where they tried to ban Catholic worship and impose a Puritan theocracy.

The Puritans were not the only people who thought that imposing religious views and laws was the proper way to build their community. John Rolfe, the man who first bred that hybrid that came to be known as Virginia tobacco, began experimenting with the "weed" in 1612 for fear of being prosecuted for idleness. Dale's Code, as the first code of law in Jamestown came to be known, was as puritanical in its tone as the Mayflower Compact was. It forbade immodest dress and not observing the Sabbath. It did not allow idleness. Idle hands are the Devil's workshop.[14]

The understanding that faith could not be imposed upon people did not come easily to us. But when we finally got the point, we made it illegal both to persecute people for their faith and to use any means at all to convince people that ours was or is the true religion. We recognized that belief and manner of belief are not punishable things: freedom of religion must be a person's inalienable and inviolable right. And once we understood that freedom of religion is inviolable, we understood that freedom of will must be too. For faith is and must be accepted through an act of free will. We also understood that human beings are inviolable, precisely because they are capable of faith.

This is not to say that we gave up on faith, on our conviction that Christianity is the true religion, on the fact that God's laws are the highest laws, or that God's rights are more important than our own. Far from it, we built our society on freedom *because* our faith is so important to us. We understood that the only way in which we can truly have faith is if we freely accept it. So we decided to protect freedom in order to make faith possible. We understood that the only way to really follow divine law is freely. So we decided to protect freedom to make it possible for people to embrace God's law freely. We chose the high road; the road of true conversion.

To make a long story short, we understood that the basis upon which we could build a just and even religious society lay not in force, as much as one might want to justify that force in the name of one's faith in God, but in the sacredness and inviolability of the human person.

American Faith and Freedom

This point, the understanding that a just society can only be based on the sacredness and inviolability of the human person, is the heart and soul of the American dream. Our nation was built upon the belief that every individual human person is sacred and inviolable: "We hold these truths to be self-evident, that all men are created equal, and endowed by the Creator with certain inalienable rights, which include life, liberty, and the pursuit of happiness." It was built upon the belief that no one — no human being, that is — can dictate to us who we are to be or what we are to do, but that it is our personal duty and responsibility to discover who we are, where our talents lie, and how we are to pursue our happiness. It was built upon the belief that each of us has a personal relation to the Creator, of which no one can strip us, as well as a personal responsibility to the Creator, from which no one can release us. It was built upon the belief that the only way to build that "City on the Hill" — which the Puritans, the Catholics, and the Quakers all dreamed of — was by allowing all people to take responsibility for themselves, for their lives, as they stood naked before God.

Three
The Responsibility of Freedom

I have a recurring nightmare, or perhaps *daymare* is the more appropriate term for it. It returns every time I walk into a classroom and face the thirty-odd people to whom I am supposed to teach something abstruse like how to demonstrate that the human soul is immaterial, or what the difference between dualism and hylomorphism is. I can get people to repeat what I am saying without their *understanding* what I am saying, why it is important, what it means to them, how to apply it, how to reason; I can get people to parrot what I am saying without their loving what I am teaching.

This is the nightmare of every professor, and it boils down to this: To teach is not just to transmit data or information. It is also to transmit ideas, ideals, love, responsibility, and things of this sort, but there is no direct and foolproof way of transmitting any of these things. Students can refuse to do the extra mile — to think things through, to understand them. And if they do refuse to think things through, there is nothing anyone can do to transmit ideals, love, and responsibility to them. This is why teaching is an art and not just a science.

It is also the nightmare of all parents. They watch their children grow up, hoping that they will do what is right, for the sake of what is right, when the time comes for them to make their own decisions and choices. They hope that their children will never lose their smiles and the joy of doing things. Yet parents know just how precarious their children's smiles and joy are; they know that things can go wrong, that good children can grow into mean and dissatisfied adults.

We can hope for our children and students. We can give them the information and examples that we think they will need in order to be great adults. But we cannot know and love what is right for our children and students. We cannot choose to do the right thing on behalf of our children and students. We cannot understand things, love things, or make choices for other people. We cannot be adults for other people. All we can do is show them what good choices are, why good choices are important, and hope that they will understand this, love this, and want to put it into practice. We hope that they will want to be good people.

This is also our country's nightmare. The downside of our protecting freedom is that we must accept the fact that people have to make their own choices. The downside of our being built upon the conviction that human beings are sacrosanct is that we must accept that we cannot violate people in order to get them to make good choices. We cannot take away the freedom of those who would make bad choices. The downside of our protecting the "inalienable rights of men" is that we can hope that all people will love our laws and understand them, but we cannot guarantee that they will.

It is a terrible risk to be a nation built upon freedom, upon the inalienable rights of human beings. By giving everyone the choice of what he or she will do, we are actually putting our whole nation's well-being on the shoulders of people who could very easily not use their freedom well. Being built on freedom means being built upon the hope that everyone will accept the responsibility of freedom, but having no means, really, to ensure that they do. Our nation is a lot like a family in this sense. Once children are grown, parents have no real way of ensuring that their children will act responsibly, will honor them and each other; that their families will thrive. Freedom is a dangerous thing, as so many parents learn to their chagrin.

Freedom and Laws

The root of our way of life is the paradox of freedom and laws. It is our country's oldest paradox, the paradox that made us become a democracy. Simply put, the paradox is this: Laws and freedom seem to be mutually exclusive things. Laws impose a certain way of life, a certain manner of doing things, upon all people; they dictate what one must not do and what one must do. Freedom, on the other hand, is, or at least seems to be, quite the opposite thing. Freedom involves making one's own choices; deliberating on how to live and deciding what one is to do. Activities like these presuppose that people are not told what they must do and what they must not do. Actually, if there are laws that dictate what one must do, there would seem to be no room for freedom. So how does one put together laws and freedom? This is our problem.

The simple answer would seem to be that a community or nation built on freedom would have no laws at all — that it would not and could not claim that there are certain things that all people must do and certain others that no one must do — since freedom cannot, it would seem, survive under laws or limitations of any sort. Is this not the position some of the people in our justice system seem to take today when they protect choices simply because they are choices, independently of their consequences? When they claim that any interference in our ability to make choices limits our freedom?[15]

But this is impossible. We need laws if we are to live together. Laws are the backbone of society; they protect the innocent against the less so, they guide one's relations to others. Without laws, all behavior becomes acceptable. But all human behavior cannot be acceptable. Human beings are capable of doing things that are harmful, both to themselves and to others. We can murder, steal, torture, enslave. And since we are capable of doing these things, it cannot be right not to state that these things should not be done. It cannot be right not to have a body of laws that hold people accountable for doing things that are wrong. This would undermine what allows a community to be a community, what allows people to live together, work together, trust each other. How can people live together if there is no law that states that one cannot murder? Without laws, people could up and kill their neighbor with impunity when they became angry. And it is quite obvious that people cannot live together if they kill each other. They cannot work together if they do not trust each other, and there is no foundation for their trust if there is no set of rules that they must all abide by.

So we have a paradox. On the one hand our attempt to build a community, a nation, on freedom would seem to be impossible to do with laws, since laws, it would seem, strangle freedom. On the other hand, it is impossible to build a nation or a community of any sort without laws. So how exactly do we build a nation on freedom? Is it not a contradiction to build a community, a nation, upon freedom?

Building a Community of Believers

We have spent some four hundred years trying to understand how to solve this paradox. It is the paradox, the challenge, on which our nation was founded. When the Pilgrims and Puritans came to our country "for the Glory of God and the Advancement of the Christian Faith," as the Mayflower Compact puts it, it was in the name of freedom — religious freedom. They wanted the freedom to live their faith as they, and not the English Crown, saw fit. They also wanted to build God's kingdom on earth, to build the "City on the Hill." They wanted everyone to follow God's laws. And their leaders were not afraid to impose respect for God's laws on people in order to build this city.

They quickly realized that there was a contradiction in their dream. The first vociferous arguments that heated the Massachusetts Bay Colony took place a mere eight years after its foundation. The heart of the arguments was precisely the matter of the relation between free will and the law in the constitution of a Christian community. John Winthrop, who was the governor of the colony at the time, was a theocrat of sorts. He was convinced that a Christian community could only be grounded in strong laws and stronger enforcement. Winthrop believed both in the power of law and law enforcement. The laws he had in mind were divine laws. The antinomians, like Roger Williams and Anne Hutchinson, claimed that a Christian community could not be grounded either in laws or in their enforcement. They asserted that the only thing that mattered when it came to faith — which is the backbone of a Christian community, after all — is one's personal relation to God. And, they claimed, the "inner light" of faith is not something that can be imposed or even bestowed upon people through laws precisely because it is God's gift. Laws, they contended, can at best be social things, but they have nothing to do with faith. Faith can only be accepted freely. Freedom, they claimed, is more important than laws when it comes to building a Christian community.

The matter at hand did not only have to do with religion; it had enormous political repercussions precisely because the Puritans were trying to construct the "City on the Hill," which is a political entity after all. Everyone was aware of this at the time. At the 1637 elections in the Massachusetts Bay Colony, the theocrats and the antinomians came face to face, and the people were called upon to choose between the two. Did they want laws to be the basis of their Christian community, or did they want freedom to be the basis of their Christian community?

On the face of things, it would seem that the Bay Colonists stood unquestionably in favor of theocracy over antinomianism, of laws over freedom. Winthrop won the election by a landslide. The antinomians, with their talk of "inner lights," gave everyone the impression that they did not believe in laws or any other product of reason for that matter, but wanted everything, politics included, to rest upon inspiration. This was not to anyone's liking. Inspiration is a private thing, which varies from person to person, and private things, which also happen to vary from person to person they felt, cannot serve as the basis for a social order, let alone the social order of a New Jerusalem. And this view of the Puritans as people who stood for the law over freedom fits in nicely with our vision of their way of life. We have read Hawthorne and seen Arthur Miller's *The Crucible.*

But this is just the face of things. In reality, the Bay Colonists were not really keen on pure theocracies — law over freedom — any more than they were on antinomian societies — placing freedom before the law. Winthrop, it is true, did become governor of the Bay Colony and brought with him stern laws and the expectation of obedience. But he did not become governor because he imposed his view of the best way to build a Christian society upon the Bay Colony. He did not *compel* the Bay Colonists to give laws precedence over freedom, which is what would have had to happen in a pure theocracy, in a community where law takes precedence over freedom. No, Winthrop became governor because the Bay Colonists *chose* to put him in power. They elected him. They also deposed him every time they saw fit.

Winthrop's career was rocky. He was stripped of the governorship almost as many times as he was elected. He ran into trouble with the people and with the preachers. The trouble with the people was an old bone of contention. The Bay Colony's charter called for a meeting of the General Court, a kind of parliament, at least four times a year. Winthrop did not find that this was necessary. In his first term as governor, 1630–34, he only called a meeting once. His high-handedness was not to the people's liking. They deposed Winthrop in 1634. They reelected him in 1637, to be sure; anything, it seems, was better than the antinomians and what the Bay Colonists perceived to be their strange mixture of purely human laws and divine illumination. But they deposed Winthrop again in 1640 because of financial problems. Finances, then as now, were taken by many to be a sign of God's favor or lack thereof. In 1642, they elected Winthrop to be governor once again. But they stripped him of his governorship again in 1644, this time because of his religious imperiousness. Winthrop had run into trouble with a preacher named Samuel Gorton, who had been spewing brimstone and hellfire against him. Winthrop responded by clapping him in irons and having him exiled. The people did not like this either, and deposed him once again.

The point is that the Bay Colonists may not have liked antinomians, since they left too much to free will. But they did not altogether like theocrats either, since they cut free will out of the civil-religious picture. They may not have liked antinomians, since they seemed to want to sunder law from faith thereby making the state "irreligious." The colonists knew that they could not live without law or faith, laws and freedom, or to be precise, without making their laws coherent with their faith. But they also knew that they needed some distinction between the public and the private, between the law and faith. What they wanted was a free city on the hill. They wanted a combination of theocracy and antinomianism, of laws and freedom.

What is more, they wanted both good leaders, whom they were willing to obey, and a voice in the matter of how all of these things would be combined in the "City on the Hill." This is why they took direct interest in Winthrop's doings after they elected him, and deposed him whenever they saw fit.

The Bay Colonists may not have liked Williams, his point about the "inner light of faith" or about the separation of church and state, but they had this much in common with him at least: they wanted to choose how they were governed, and they ensured that their government was in place through their free and voluntary consent. Their consent was necessary. It was what ensured that they kept religious freedom, the need for which brought them to this country in the first place.

Freedom and Democracy

What the early adventures of the Massachusetts Bay Colony illustrate are the roots of our solution to the paradox of building a community on freedom. Our ancestors realized that if a society as a whole defines and freely accepts its civil laws, then these laws cannot contradict or negate that individual freedom that is necessary to build a society founded on freedom, precisely because it is the society as a whole that defines and freely accepts them; if society as a whole freely appoints — and monitors — its government, then the members of that society do not forsake their freedom by obeying their government precisely because they have freely appointed their government and freely keep it in place through their consent.

This solution is called democracy: the rule of the people, or rule through popular consent. It is an ingenious solution to the paradox of freedom and the law. By making the government rest upon popular consent, democracy does not allow a government to impose laws upon the people. It thereby allows people to maintain their freedom while living under laws. It also sets up the ideal situation for having good laws. For one would hope that a people as a whole would not consent to live under bad laws. By making the government's power rest upon popular consent, one gives the people the means to resist bad laws. They can simply withhold their consent to the government any time it tries to pass a bad law.

This is not only what the Bay Colonists had in mind in their tug-of-war with John Winthrop, it is also what the Founding Fathers had in mind when they wrote our Constitution. The foundation of any just government, they were convinced, must be the consent of the governed, because it is intrinsically wrong to impose a government upon a people: "The fabric of the American empire ought to rest on the solid basis of *the consent of the people.* The streams of national power ought to flow immediately from that pure, original fountain of all legitimate authority."[16] This is why they did the unheard-of thing of having the Constitution ratified by popular vote. Our nation, they would affirm, time and time again, had to be formed freely by the people so that all could be governed by just law: "The body-politic is formed by a voluntary association of individuals. It is a social compact, by which the whole people covenants with each citizen, and each citizen with the whole people, that all shall be governed by certain laws for the common good."[17]

Democracy came naturally to us. This is the miracle of our country. What contributed to it was not just our Christianity, although Christianity was arguably its most important cause.[18] Democracy was also a product of our English inheritance and that general tendency in the English to push for various forms of governmental representation that first led them to form a parliament in the thirteenth century. By the time our ancestors first came to this country the *Magna Carta* had long been signed.

The immense amount of land that our ancestors settled also contributed to our becoming a democracy. Many of the immigrants who came to our country did so for the freedom that it afforded. They came because they could never have owned their own land nor had the opportunity to prosper in their native countries. This was true from the very beginning. But to allow people to possess their own land, and to put their talents to use as they see fit, is to give them a freedom that cannot sit well with anything but a democracy. Once one begins to make one's own decisions, one does not want others to tell one what one should do. Individual thinking and decision making does not sit well with feudal systems, viceroys, or dictates emanating from monarchs who live on faraway continents. "The basic economic fact about the New World was that land was plentiful: it was labor and skills that were in short supply. To get immigrants you had to offer them land, and once they arrived they were determined to become individual entrepreneurs, subject to no one but the law.... People spread out to the interior, out of control of everything except the law, which they respected and generally observed. But they had to make the law themselves."[19] So Americans quickly set up "houses of representatives" in each of the original thirteen colonies. In them, they could voice their own concerns and participate in their government. The oldest of these, the House of Burgesses, dated back to 1619. They also wrote constitutions.

American colonies not only had parliaments long before most European countries did, they also had written constitutions before them all, with the possible exception of tiny Italian republics like the Repubblica di San Marino. The first constitution was the *Fundamental Orders of Connecticut*. It was written in 1639. And most colonists abided by their constitutions. They knew them, changed them, expanded them. Most Americans took self-governance seriously, and meant by self-governance the practice of understanding and defining the law: "Having a constitution inevitably led you to think in terms of rights, natural law, and absolutes, things the English were conditioned... not to trouble their heads about. That was 'abstract stuff.' But it was not abstract for Americans."[20] So seriously did the colonists take their right to self-governance that when the English Crown decided to wrestle control of the colonies from their hands, it found that it was unable to do so. Americans, they discovered, were willing to fight an eight-year war for their freedom.

The Perils of Democracy

Although democracies are a solution to the paradox of building a community, a nation, on freedom, they are not a foolproof solution. There is a reason why many European countries shied away from democracy until very recently. The democracies of European history were volatile. They were rife with problems and did not, as a rule, last: "This fact stems, of course, from the instability specific to this form of political organization. Civil strife between factions often led to the paralysis and even self-destruction of the city-state, as the chronicles of the Greek and Italian city-states eloquently attest."[21]

Athens, the first of all democracies, was not a stable one. The government of Athens swung back and forth between democracy and tyranny for years, until Alexander the Great put an end to Athens's self-rule altogether. Italian city-states of the Middle Ages and Renaissance were just as temperamental. They often had to call in a foreigner to act as their executive power because the democratic factions could not get along. Ancient Rome was, it is true, a republic for a very long time. The fact of the matter is, however, that democracy did not last there either. Rome became a monarchy as soon as its empire began to expand seriously. Venice was a republic, and died a republic, *a serene republic.* But Venice too felt that it had to limit its democracy once its empire began to expand. It became an oligarchy.

There are two almost insurmountable barriers that democracies have to overcome in order to work. The first is our natural tendency to pursue our personal interests over those of our society as a whole. Both history and our own experience show just how difficult this is. We are a fallen race. And the simple, brutal truth is that democracies do not work if every member of a people — or at east the great majority of the nation — does not feel responsible for that nation as a whole.

The moment that people do not consider themselves personally responsible for their nation and stop caring for their nation, the nation loses its cohesiveness and begins to split into tiny groups of people who want to promote their own personal agendas. These groups become factions, which begin to fight one another in order to impose their agendas upon one another. It is thus that a democracy can turn into an oligarchy, in which a few stronger parties, which have defeated the weaker ones, band together to control the nation and impose their agenda upon it. This is what happened in Venice at the turn of the thirteenth century. Or a nation can turn into a monarchy if one of the factions that vies for power is significantly stronger than all of the others. This is what happened in France once the violent storm of the French Revolution began to subside. That was when Napoleon had himself elected First-Consul (i.e., dictator) for life, and then he decided to have himself crowned emperor. It is also what happened in Rome.

The second problem with democracies is that they require all of their members to have a clear understanding of both the purpose of their union — the immediate and long-term goals of their nation and its underlying values — and of the roles that they must play in order to promote their nation's short- and long-term goals and for the nation to attain its purpose.

In absolute monarchies, it is the monarch who dictates what the people as a whole are to do, the long- and short-term goals of the nation as a whole, and the roles that people can and cannot play in furthering those goals. This is the monarch's role. When Queen Isabella of Castile decided that it was of paramount importance for Spain to complete her liberation from the Moors by ensuring that she harbored no secret enemies, she set up the Inquisition. She appointed the people who were to conduct the Inquisition. She deferred to no one in this choice. The burden of having set up the Inquisition rests on her shoulders alone. When King Henry VIII decided that England would no longer be Catholic, he made it obligatory for all of his subjects to renounce their Catholicism. His decision was his alone; he set the course of English history. The responsibility of that decision rests with him alone.

In a democracy there is (or should be) no single person who determines the short- and long-term goals of the nation, no single person on whose shoulders the fate of the nation rests. If they are to be a democracy, the people as a whole must determine these goals, it is the people who must come to a common understanding of those goals. What is more, in a democracy no one can (or should be able to) impose a role upon anyone else, no one should be able to dictate what another adult must do. Democracies call people to understand their own roles in the nation as a whole; how they are to further the goals of their nation, what they can and cannot do.

Both of these conditions are obvious. If a democracy is formed through the consent of the people, then if that consent is lacking — because people are not interested in their nation or because they cannot agree on what the nation should be or do — there can be no democracy. Both conditions are extremely difficult to attain.

How does one make all members of a nation feel responsible for the well-being of the nation as a whole? How does one make all members of a nation understand the purpose of their nation; its long- and short-term goals? How does one make all members of a nation want to play the part in it that they, and not their vanity, can and should play? Obviously, if a democracy is to be a democracy, the answer is that one cannot. The responsibility for the nation, the understanding of its goals, and one's role in the furtherance of these goals, must either arise from within each member of a democratic nation, or it cannot exist at all. This is what makes democracy an almost impossible ideal.

The Responsibility of Democracy

Impossible or not, democracy is the one way we have to solve that paradox on which our nation was founded. If we really want to be a nation built on freedom, on those *inalienable rights* that we believe all people self-evidently have — the rights to "life, liberty, and the pursuit of happiness" — then we have to be a nation grounded in the free consent of all citizens. And if we are to be grounded in consent, we have to be a democracy. The only real way of protecting our freedom is by being a democracy, by accepting responsibility for our nation.

Nations do need laws. And laws can limit personal freedom. There are no two ways about this. The only way that laws cannot and do not limit personal freedom is for us freely to accept those laws, to understand them, and to take part in defining them. What this means, of course, is that the only way to solve that paradox on which our nation was founded is for us all to accept that we are responsible for the well-being of our nation as a whole. That is what freely accepting our laws, understanding our laws, and defining our laws is all about.

We could choose to do none of these things. It is easy to think of ourselves as insignificant pieces of a world that is much too big for us to control and shy back to our televisions and things that we can control. It is also easy to think of ourselves as God's gift to the universe, beings to whom the world owes something, and who owe nothing to the world. It is easy to break the rules, to claim that there are no such things as rules, or to think of ourselves as exceptions to the rules. But the sad fact is that if we do any of these things, we cannot really be the land of the free.

If we do not actively understand what our laws are, actively accept them, and move to change them when they are wrong, those laws will be an unbearable burden on our shoulders. We will do everything to escape them and end up losing our freedom, because no nation can exist without laws. If too many of us do not understand our laws, accept our laws, sit back and do not push for just laws, there will be nothing to ensure that people do respect human rights. And if people do not respect human rights, we cannot be a nation built on freedom.

There is nothing we can do to force everyone to understand our laws, accept them, and define them. This is why it is such a risk to be built on freedom. Like students in a classroom, citizens of our nation can refuse to go the extra mile. Like adult members of a family, citizens of our nation can refuse to accept the responsibility of freedom. But if there are enough of us who do accept responsibility for our nation, the project can work.

Four

The Limits of Freedom

There is a wonderful scene in a movie called *The American President* in which Michael Douglas, who plays the part of the president of the United States, a president who is trying to bolster his plummeting poll ratings, goes into a tirade. If we want to be American and really stand for liberty, he claims, we cannot silence people. We have to accept that there are people who are going to say things that make our blood boil, and we have to let them say what they will. Being American, he continues, does not just mean defending the flag or applauding those who would sing their praises of our country. It also means letting those who would burn our flag in protest show their discontent, just as it means letting those who would batter America while living in this country, as citizens of this country, say what they please. Being American, he claims, means giving the protection of our Bill of Rights not just to those with whom we agree, but also to those with whom we do not agree, those whom we would spend a lifetime trying to disprove. America, the scene concludes, is about *advanced citizenship.*

There is something right about this. We are the land of the free. We are built upon the belief that there is something sacred about human beings, that human beings have the inalienable rights to "life, liberty, and the pursuit of happiness." And if we are to do anything more than just give lip service to our beliefs, we have to acknowledge that people have the right to speak their minds freely, believe freely, write freely, publish what they want, assemble freely, and defend their freedom. We have to admit that we cannot silence people without limiting their freedom. We cannot tell people what they are to think or what they are to do without contradicting our ideals.

We have come to think that chaos and cacophony are the price that we must pay for our belief in freedom and the inalienability of human rights. Since we cannot impose opinions on people, any opinion must be acceptable; since we must accept that people have the right to form their own beliefs, all beliefs must be acceptable; since we must recognize that everyone can say anything, there is nothing that cannot be said. We have come to think that there are no limits to personal freedom, so long as people do not physically harm someone whom our laws recognize to be human persons through their freedom.

The Supreme Court has gone a long way to promote this view in the last fifty years. It has taken the First Amendment to sanction people's right to assemble and march in the name of the most appalling things. I am thinking here of things like its having allowed Neo-Nazis to demonstrate in the town of Skokie, Illinois, which has a large number of Jewish Holocaust survivors. It has taken the First Amendment to sanction people's right to publish the most execrable things, such as falsehoods and child pornography. The Supreme Court has claimed that every citizen has the right to define what is right, what life is, what the meaning of life is, implicitly holding that all opinions regarding these matters must be equally acceptable: "At the heart of liberty is the right to define one's own concept of existence, of meaning, of the universe, and of the mystery of human life. Beliefs about these matters could not define the attributes of personhood were they formed under the compulsion of the State."[22] There is a sense in which the Supreme Court must be right with respect to all of these things. If we are the land of the free, we cannot impose opinions or actions on people. What this means, of course, is that we must allow people to form their own concepts regarding all of the most important things in life and to act in the way they see fit. If we are the land of the free, we must allow people to choose what to do and to do as they choose.

James Madison made this point very clearly in the *Federalist Papers*. Whatever one might want to do to ensure that a nation be united, he claimed, one cannot impose upon "every citizen the same opinions, the same passions, and the same interests." This cure for disunity is "worse than the disease." It is a negation of personal liberty, and "It could not be less folly to abolish liberty, which is essential to political life, because it nourishes faction, than it would be to wish the annihilation of air, which is essential to animal life, because it imparts to fire its destructive agency."[23] Madison held that it is intrinsically wrong to *force* all people to believe and to do the same things in the same way, not only because it is counterproductive, although it certainly is. "In politics, as in religion, it is equally absurd to aim at making proselytes by fire and sword. Heresies in either can rarely be cured by persecution."[24] It is wrong, he thought, because it would be a violation of human beings, of those "faculties from which the right to property originates," to force opinions on them.

To be the land of the free also means to be the land of free thinkers and free doers. This much is clear. But here is the problem. Does being the land of free thinkers and doers also entail that we all have to accept everyone's opinions and all beliefs? That we all have to accept every concept of existence formulated by any person in any circumstance? Does being the land of the free entail that we have to allow anyone to do anything because we must respect everyone's *inalienable* rights to "life, liberty, and the pursuit of happiness"? Does being the land of the free mean that everything goes? Are there no limits to our freedom?

It would seem to me that defending freedom cannot mean this. To claim that people must respect any opinion, or that all beliefs are acceptable, is as excessive as forcing every person to hold the same opinions, the same beliefs. Like cultural indoctrination of the kind that Madison warned against, it forces opinions on people. And like that cultural indoctrination, it violates human rights, those "faculties from which the right to property originates."

Beliefs and the Freedom of Thinkers

Let's be honest. None of us, really, holds that all beliefs are acceptable, not if we have any beliefs, that is. We cannot even hold a belief if we also believe that all beliefs are acceptable. In order to believe that all beliefs are acceptable, we would also have to believe that those beliefs that hold our own beliefs as false are also acceptable. But we could not have any beliefs if we believed that those beliefs that hold our beliefs as false are acceptable. The condition of holding or accepting any belief is the belief that that belief is true. And we could not believe that our beliefs are true if we also held that those beliefs that claim that our beliefs are false are also true. So we would not have any beliefs if we believed that all beliefs are acceptable. When we claim "I believe in one God," it is because the claim that "God exists" seems inherently true. But if we believe that the claim "God exists" is inherently true, then we cannot also believe that it is inherently not true. If this is so and if a condition of accepting a belief is recognizing its truthfulness, then we cannot possibly accept that belief that claims that "God exists" is not inherently true, if we do believe in one God. Not without giving up our initial belief, that is. So the moment that we have any beliefs at all, we also have to believe that there is a set of beliefs that we cannot accept, a set of unacceptable beliefs.

If I believe that it is "self-evident that all men are created equal," I cannot also believe that it is "not self-evident that all men are created equal" or that it is "self-evident that all men are not created equal." The beliefs that "it is true that it is self-evident that all men are created equal" and that "it is true that men are created equal" are part and parcel of my belief that "it is self-evident that all men are created equal." They are the reason why I accept the belief that it is "self-evident that all men are created equal." So I could not possibly believe that "it is not self-evident that all men are created equal" or that "it is self-evident that all men are not created equal" are true if I believe that "it is self-evident that all men are created equal." What this means is that I could not accept these beliefs without losing my original belief. I would either have to lie to myself or be schizophrenic to believe that "it is not self-evident that all men are created equal" or that "it is self-evident that all men are not created equal" are true beliefs while I believe that it is "self-evident that all men are created equal." I would have to negate my own rationality in order to believe that these beliefs are acceptable. As this is true of my belief concerning the equality of men, so is it true of many of my other beliefs. The moment that we really believe something, we cannot believe that all beliefs are acceptable. Not if we want to respect ourselves.

But if we cannot have any beliefs at all if we believe that all beliefs are acceptable, then for someone to claim that we have to accept *all* beliefs — which naturally includes those beliefs that contradict our own — is for that person to violate our right to hold our own beliefs. It is to violate those "faculties from which the right to property originates." We could not think coherently or believe anything if we were to believe that those beliefs that we believe to be true are false, which is what we would have to do if we were to have to accept all beliefs.

This may sound harsh and undemocratic. After all, we are all entitled to our own beliefs and to express them as we will. This is a free country. So why can we not live and let live, think and let think? Why can we not let all people be right in their own little world? Do we have to be so mean-spirited about beliefs?

We could let all people be right in their own little world, and many people want to claim that there is nothing wrong with this. Perhaps they are right. But once individuals start expressing their opinions and beliefs, publishing their opinions and beliefs, or communicating with any one of us, they have stepped outside the boundaries of their own little world and have entered a world to which we all belong. And in this bigger world, we all have opinions and beliefs that could contradict theirs. Anything they say could contradict our beliefs. For them to expect us to listen to them, to entertain a conversation with them, and to accept their beliefs, as such, could allow them to violate our own rights as free thinkers to be free to believe what we want to believe.

Freedom and Society

This points to yet another paradox at the root of our way of life: Freedom and society seem to be mutually exclusive things. There are two principal reasons for this. The first is that the unlimited exercise of freedom is a practical impossibility when one lives in a society. The second is that the unlimited exercise of freedom undermines the unity of a society.

It is a practical impossibility for all members of a society to have unlimited freedom. The problems intrinsic in free speech illustrate this beautifully. If we want to claim that all individuals have the inalienable rights to "life, liberty, and the pursuit of happiness," and mean by that that there are no limits to people's freedom, we would seem thereby to have to claim that all opinions and beliefs, all ways of life, all manner of pursuing happiness are acceptable. After all, all opinions and beliefs are necessarily formulated by persons who have the inalienable right to think what they want, and are necessarily expressed by persons who can say what they want; every way of life is lived by persons who have the inalienable right to pursue happiness as they see fit. Claiming that some beliefs are inadequate — or unacceptable — or that some ways of life should not be pursued is to claim that there are limits to people's freedom, and to claim that there are limits to people's freedom, it would seem, is a breach of people's inalienable rights. The problem is that not putting limits on people's freedom is to violate those very rights that we are trying to protect by not putting limits on freedom. If all individuals are entitled not only to their own opinions and beliefs but also to express them at will, and to expect that their opinions and beliefs will be accepted by people other than themselves, they will violate the rights of these other people, the rights of their listeners, who may or may not want to accept their beliefs, because they too have beliefs of their own, which may or may not be in accord with the beliefs of the speaker. These people also have the right to believe what they want, and expressing opinions and beliefs and expecting others to accept their opinions and beliefs simply because they have the right to their own beliefs will violate those rights.

Defending the inalienable right to liberty, if by that one means unlimited freedom, leads to a contradiction. If we want to protect people's inalienable rights to "liberty and the pursuit of happiness," then we would seem bound to claim that everyone must accept all opinions, beliefs, and ways of life. But claiming that everyone must accept all opinions, beliefs, and ways of life is also to violate people's inalienable rights, just as claiming that someone must listen to any opinion or belief and think about another person's opinion or belief is a breach of that person's inalienable rights. So how exactly are we to respect the human right to free thought? How are we to be the land of free thinkers and doers if being the land of free thinkers and doers means both that we must allow all people to think what they want and that we cannot be expected to accept anything that anyone thinks since denying either thing would violate our right to think freely? Is it not somewhat of a contradiction to build a nation upon human rights, upon the unlimited exercise of freedom? Are freedom and society not mutually exclusive?

The way out of this paradox would seem to be to claim that all people have the right to hold their own opinions and beliefs and to express them, but do not have the right to expect other people to listen to, think about, or accept their opinions and beliefs. After all, if no one needs to listen to other people's opinions or beliefs, think about them, or accept them, then everyone's having their own opinions and beliefs cannot violate anyone's inalienable rights. The problems entailed by everyone's being entitled to form their own opinions and beliefs, in other words, arise once people express their opinions and beliefs and expect other people to listen to them and to believe them. It is when they express them, and expect others to believe them, that they can violate other people's rights. So we could avoid the problems inherent in free speech altogether if we did not expect anyone to listen or to believe other people's opinions and beliefs.

But there is a problem with this solution. If we are all entitled to believe anything we want and are not expected in any way to listen to what another person is saying or to believe it, then none of us can work together to form a community. Working together, living together, and belonging to a single society entail both listening to others and believing what they are saying to some degree. How could I work with my assistant if he did not have to listen to what I am saying or could think anything he wanted about the tasks that I assign him? He could think that I did not assign him those tasks and not perform them. And I would have no recourse against this if he did not have to listen to me. How could I live by my next-door neighbors if they did not listen to me or believe me when I told them that my computer is mine and not theirs, and that I therefore did not want them to take it away from me? How could I convince people that I am a rational human being who has the inalienable rights to life, liberty, and the pursuit of happiness if people did not have to listen to anything I say and could believe what they want about those things that I do say? If people did not have to listen to me, they could declare me irrational and deprive me of my rights.

This illustrates the second reason why freedom and society seem to be mutually exclusive things: The unlimited exercise of freedom undermines the foundations of the unity of a society. There is no foundation for our communication if we do not have to listen to one another or accept each other's opinions and beliefs. There is no foundation for communication if we all are entitled to believe what we want. But if we want to claim that we can all think what we want without restrictions, that our freedom of thought is unlimited, then we are going to have to claim both that no one has to listen to anyone else and that anyone is entitled to believe *anything* they want. What this means is that there can be no foundation for communication if everyone's freedom of thought is unlimited. But if being built upon unlimited freedom of thought entails not having a foundation for communication, it would seem impossible for a society to be built upon un-limited freedom of thought. A community is formed through communication.

So what exactly are we to do with free speech and free thought? How can we be *one* nation of a multitude of *diverse* people with *diverse* opinions if we must let all everyone believe what they want? The paradox of free speech goes straight to the foundations of our democracy. It would seem to imply that one person's exercise of freedom necessarily limits an-other's and consequently that no one can exercise freedom in a land that is grounded in everyone's inalienable right to be free. What holds for free speech, after all, holds for free acts of all kinds. It would also seem to imply that a nation grounded in freedom cannot be a nation at all. Freedom and society seem to be mutually exclusive things.

Beliefs and the Foundations of Communities

There are some beliefs to which all members of a commu-nity must assent in order to form a community. These are the beliefs that make communication between human beings possible, that establish the rules of communication. They in-clude beliefs about a good number of things that range from the conventional meaning of words, to the rules of logic, to a set of principles that define a set of basic values that all those who would communicate with each other must respect. The clearer and more extensive these shared beliefs are, the more thoroughly people can communicate and the more unified a community can be.

There are quite a few contemporary psychological studies that deal precisely with this point. These studies indicate that much of the friction that exists in married couples stems from the different ways in which men and women often use words, the different ways in which they often think.[25] The classic example that illustrates this point is a conversation between a husband and wife who are driving on the highway. "Should we stop at the next gas station?" asks the wife. The husband responds, "I am not tired." Dialogues like these sound nonsensical and often end up in fights. "I am not tired" is clearly not an expected response to the question "Should we stop at the next gas station?" The expected responses are statements like "Yes," "No," or "I don't know." And since "I am not tired" is not an anticipated response to the question, "Should we stop at the next gas station?" it can prompt responses like, "That is not what I was asking," to which a whole series of answers like "Yes it was" can ensue.

Why the odd response? The husband who said "I am not tired" clearly believed that by asking whether they should stop at the gas station, his wife was not just asking whether or not they should stop at the station. He thought that she was asking whether he was tired and was giving a direct answer to that question. But why did he think that his wife was asking whether he was tired when the question she asked was "Should we stop at the next gas station?" He interpreted the question this way partly because his wife did not ask him what she really wanted to ask. "Should we stop at the next gas station?" is a good example of an indirect question. It does not state whether or not the person who asks the question wants to stop at a gas station or thinks that it is a good idea to stop at a gas station. The wife did not say, "I would like to stop at the next gas station. Could we stop, please?" or "I think we should stop at the next gas station. Could we stop, please?" Nor does the question state why the wife might think that they should stop at a gas station. "Could we stop, please? I am tired." "I think we are running low on gas. Should we stop?" The question only implies that the person who is asking the question might have some reason for wanting to stop.

The reason why exchanges like this one can end up in fights is that the husband and wife in the example have different rules of communication. The husband clearly believed that when one communicates one should state what one thinks, rather than allude to it. That is why he cut to the chase and responded directly to the indirect question that he thought his wife was asking. The wife, on the other hand, used an indirect way of communicating. Rather than stating exactly what she thought, she hinted at it through a question. The husband and wife had different basic beliefs, regarding the proper manner of speaking. And it is precisely because they had different basic beliefs on this matter that they risked a fight. When people have different basic beliefs their communication is impaired, and where there is impaired communication, fights can arise.

The problem that this example illustrates does not just exist with married couples. It exists in relations of all sorts: cross-cultural relations, cross-generational relations, cross-faith relations. Different basic beliefs impede communication. Just how much they do so depends upon the level of difference between these beliefs and the sorts of basic beliefs that differ. The husband and wife in the example had different basic beliefs with respect to some rules of communication. The husband believed that communication should be direct. The wife did not. But they had other common beliefs: that words have specific meanings, that one should communicate, that one should communicate with words, that words represent thoughts, that they did not want to harm one another. The differences in their basic beliefs are what could have caused them to misunderstand one another. Their common basic beliefs are what could have allowed them to overcome their misunderstanding. If differences in basic beliefs are not complete, two people can communicate. They can build a relation. If two people have no basic beliefs in common, they cannot communicate. They cannot build a relation of any sort. As this holds for two people, it clearly holds for a community as a whole — a plurality of persons. In order for people to form a community, they must be able to communicate with one another. In order to communicate, they must have a common set of basic beliefs.

Common Beliefs and American Values

The real questions when it comes to our nation are whether or not we can have a common set of basic beliefs and what kind of beliefs these can be. These questions are a consequence of the fact that we want to defend human rights and of the way that we have come to view freedom. If we are all free and if freedom entails that we each can form whatever beliefs we want, it would seem plausible to claim that we cannot expect all Americans to have a common set of basic beliefs. Many people seem to make this very claim when they state that all beliefs must be acceptable in America. That every American has the right to define what is right, what life is, what the meaning of life is. The conclusion that they draw from this claim is that there can be no basic values and ends to which our entire nation consents. That America can only have individual values and ends that are determined by each individual American.[26] But this is precisely the problem. If Americans only have individual values and ends, we will not and cannot have a common set of basic beliefs. And if we cannot have a common set of basic beliefs, there can be no such thing as America, a single nation formed of a plurality of persons. If we all have different basic beliefs, we will not be able to communicate with one another. If we cannot communicate with one another, we cannot coordinate our efforts, pursue a common goal, live by and with each other. And if we cannot do any of these things, we cannot form a community, a nation. This is why it seems to be such a contradiction to ground a nation in freedom. Freedom or, better yet, the attempt to build a nation on freedom seems to preclude the possibility of people's having a common set of basic beliefs. If everyone must be allowed to think anything he wants, which is what freedom seems to entail, none of us, it would seem, will have the same beliefs. And if we don't have the same beliefs, we cannot have a common set of basic beliefs. With no common set of basic beliefs, we cannot be a nation.

But is it really true that the attempt to build the land of the free precludes people's having a common set of basic beliefs? It would seem to me that it cannot. In order for freedom to preclude people's having a common set of basic beliefs, the attempt itself to build the land of the free — or to live in the land of the free — must not presuppose a common set of basic beliefs in all those who would build — or inhabit — the land of the free. But building — or inhabiting — the land of the free does presuppose a common set of basic beliefs in those who would build and inhabit the land of the free. It presupposes that all those people who would build or live in this land believe that freedom is a value to be pursued. It presupposes that all those who would build or live in the land of the free believe that human life is inviolable. Exercising freedom presupposes that one lives. If one wants to protect the human right to exercise freedom, as such, one must protect human life. It presupposes that those who would build or live in the land of the free believe that human beings have inalienable rights. We could not believe that human life is inviolable without claiming that human beings are inviolable, and to claim that human beings are inviolable is to claim that they have certain inalienable rights. These are just a few of the basic beliefs that the attempt to build the land of the free — or to inhabit it — presupposes in all those who would build or inhabit it. They demonstrate that far from precluding people's having a common set of basic beliefs, building or inhabiting the land of the free presupposes that people have a common set of basic beliefs.

Americans do have a common set of basic beliefs. We could not have all of the problems that we do trying to understand what we are and how we are to be what we are if we did not all share a common set of basic beliefs. Were we not to believe that human beings have the inalienable right to liberty, free speech would not be a problem for us. We would simply claim that some people cannot speak their minds and avoid the problems inherent in free speech altogether. Were we not to believe that all human beings equally share in the right to free speech, we would force part of the population to grin and bear what they have to hear and again avoid the problems inherent in free speech. The point here is simple. The paradoxes that emerge in our country with respect to the exercise of freedom result from the fact that we believe that all people have inalienable rights. It is because we all believe that thinkers of all kinds — speakers and listeners — all have inalienable rights that we find it so difficult to reconcile the rights of speakers with the rights of listeners. It is because we believe that it is "self-evident that all men are created equal, and endowed by the Creator with certain inalienable rights, which include life, liberty, and the pursuit of happiness" that we do not quite know what do with free speech. And as this is true of free speech, so is it true of all of the other issues that we discuss and disagree upon, issues that range from welfare to healthcare, censorship to abortion, taxation to foreign policies. They are problems for us too because we all agree that all human beings have the inalienable right to freedom and that all people are equal before the law. Both sides of the healthcare issue defend their positions by invoking people's inalienable rights. Those who would want the government to provide health care for all Americans claim that health is essential to life, and that the right to life is an inalienable right of all people. Thus since it is the government's job to protect people's inalienable rights, they argue, the government must provide health care to all Americans. Those who would not want the government to provide health care for all Americans do not question that the right to life inalienably belongs to all people. They also do not question that the government's job is to protect people's inalienable rights. They question the claim that the best way to protect inalienable rights is through government-run programs. Government-run health care systems, they claim, would limit people's freedom in a significant way. They would require Americans to pay a significant tax to fund a system that the taxpayers might not want to use. Most people prefer choosing their own doctors to using a government-run health care system. The right to freedom, they argue, also belongs inalienably to all people. And governmental health care systems violate that right. The point is that if we look at our present disputes and debates, we will see that we all do believe that all human beings have the inalienable rights to "life, liberty, and the pursuit of happiness." We all do have a common set of basic beliefs. We have the problems that we do precisely because we have a common set of basic beliefs, common values, and ends.

Common Beliefs and Freedom

To some, the fact that we can or even that we actually do have a common set of basic beliefs may not be enough of a reason to claim that those who would build or inhabit the land of the free *must* have a common set of beliefs. It might be true, they could claim, that those who build or inhabit the land of the free could have a common set of basic beliefs, or perhaps even that they should ideally have a common set of beliefs. But there is something contradictory about the claim that those who would build or inhabit the land of the free *must* have a common set of basic beliefs. Musts indicate necessity, and freedom and necessity are antithetical. If there are some rules with which those who would build or inhabit the land of the free must comply, then those who would build or inhabit the land of the free cannot be free to the extent that their building or inhabiting the land of the free depends upon their compliance with these rules. If their compliance is the building block of the land of the free, then the land of the free can in no way be the land of the free. It will be grounded in rules and not freedom. Thus, if those who build or inhabit the land of the free *must* have a common set of basic beliefs because their acceptance of these basic beliefs is the foundation of their nation, theirs cannot really be a nation grounded in freedom. It will be a nation grounded in rules, and rules are not freedom. There is more. By grounding a nation in rules rather than freedom, a common set of basic beliefs would also limit people's freedom. It would keep people from thinking anything they want. It would forbid people to think anything that contradicts the common set of basic beliefs. But freedom entails allowing all people to think anything they want. Thus it would seem that one cannot claim that those who would build or inhabit the land of the free must have a common set of basic beliefs. Having a common set of basic beliefs, it would seem, cannot be a prerequisite of building or inhabiting the land of the free. Freedom is what is essential to the land of the free, not beliefs.

To put the point slightly differently, the claim that those who would build or inhabit the land of the free must have a common set of basic beliefs does not specify how those who would build or inhabit the land of the free come to believe that common set of basic beliefs or the effects of their having a common set of basic beliefs. And both the cause and the effects of making a common set of basic beliefs a prerequisite of building a nation indicate that the land of the free cannot presuppose a common set of basic beliefs in all those who would build or inhabit it. To begin with, it seems impossible for all people to come freely to hold the same set of basic beliefs. People who think freely form different thoughts. Human beings are unique individuals, after all, and that uniqueness informs their thought processes. If human beings are allowed to think freely, each of them will formulate unique thoughts. And if all human beings formulate unique thoughts, it is unlikely that they will come to any common set of basic beliefs, let alone to that specific set of basic beliefs that a whole group of people needs in order to build and inhabit the land of the free. Forcing cannot be permitted in the land of the free. This is what makes it seem impossible for the land of the free to require a common set of basic beliefs in all those who would build and inhabit it. A common set of basic beliefs simply does not seem to be something that all thinkers could formulate or accept if they are allowed to think freely. If this is so, however, then if those who would build or inhabit the land of the free do have a common set of basic beliefs, it cannot be through their free thought that they come to those beliefs. If it is not through their free thought that they come to these beliefs, or so the argument goes, then they must be *forced* to believe them. But if those who would build or inhabit the land of the free must be forced to believe a common set of basic beliefs, the land of the free cannot be grounded in a common set of basic beliefs. This is why some contemporary thinkers claim that there can only be individual ends and values in land of the free. If all people must be allowed to think freely, then they must all be allowed to form their own beliefs, and the beliefs they will form will be different. We can only have individual beliefs and values in the land of the free. There is more. However people come by their common set of basic beliefs, the very fact of having to have a common set of basic beliefs puts limits on human minds. But limits and freedom are antithetical. Therefore, it would seem obvious that the land of the free cannot presuppose any set of basic beliefs in any thinker, let alone a common set of basic beliefs in all thinkers.

These objections raise two important points. The land of the free cannot presuppose a common set of basic beliefs in all those who would inhabit it if this means forcing people to assent to a common set of basic beliefs or limiting their freedom. This would violate human rights. Can we, then, really claim that America, the land of the free, cannot exist without a common set of basic beliefs simply because communities are formed through communication and communication presupposes a common set of basic beliefs? Don't basic beliefs defeat the whole point of America? They may. Then again, they may not. In order for a set of basic beliefs to be incompatible with our being the land of the free, there must be no basic beliefs to which all free thinkers must assent, and free thinkers must not be capable of freely coming to hold that common set of basic beliefs that building and inhabiting the land of the free requires. It is only if there are no basic beliefs to which we must all assent that it is contradictory to claim that all those who would build or inhabit the land of the free must have a common set of basic beliefs. It is only if we cannot all freely formulate these basic beliefs that it is contradictory to claim that those who would build or inhabit the land of the free can have a common set of basic beliefs. It is true, then, that free thinkers cannot freely formulate and assent to that common set of basic beliefs that building and inhabiting the land of the free requires? Is it true that there are no beliefs to which all free thinkers must assent?

Necessity and Freedom

There are some beliefs the acceptance of which cannot violate the rights of any free thinker. These are beliefs that a thinker already freely believes or that are implicit in that person's freely formed beliefs. If after careful reflection I freely come to believe that "Chopin is a great composer," no one can violate my rights by asking me to accept the belief that "Chopin is a great composer." That belief is one that I already have. It is a belief that I have already accepted. To ask me to accept that belief is to ask me to do what I have already freely done. Asking me to believe what I already freely believe does not violate my right to free thought. Now it could happen that there is a Chopin Lover's Club and that the one condition of joining that club is believing that "Chopin is a great composer." The rules of the club could even demand that everyone who wants to belong to that club recite a pledge of allegiance: "I hold this truth to be self-evident that Chopin is a great composer." Would joining this club impose any beliefs upon me? Would it violate my right to free thought? At first glance it might seem so. After all, it is necessary for me to hold that "Chopin is a great composer" in order to join the club — the club's rules state this very clearly — and necessity and freedom are mutually exclusive things. But this is where appearances can be deceiving. It is naturally possible that joining the club could impose beliefs on me. I could join the club without believing that "Chopin is a great composer" — because the club serves wonderful truffles — and feel forced to believe that Chopin is a great composer in order to join and eat the truffles. But how could joining the club force me to hold any belief at all, if the one belief that the club expects me to hold is that "Chopin is a great composer," and I already have come to believe that freely before I joined the club? It could not. The demand that I hold that "Chopin is a great composer" would contradict my freely holding that belief only if the demand were the only cause of my belief. But I can freely hold that "Chopin is a great composer" independently of its being required of me, or demanded of me, and still join the club where it is required of me. The point is that my holding that "Chopin is a great composer" can be both free and necessary.

As this holds for musical beliefs, so too does it hold for other beliefs. It is not said that we cannot freely come to hold required beliefs. Freedom and necessity are mutually exclusive with respect to beliefs only if we believe something, which is required of us for one reason or another, because it is required of us by something other than our belief or our reflection. But we can easily hold a belief that is in some sense necessary — that is required for some purpose or other — independently of its being required of us. If this is so, however, then it is not said that those who would build or inhabit the land of the free cannot require that all those people who would build or inhabit that land hold a belief, or even a common set of basic beliefs. It is not said that a common set of basic beliefs cannot be a prerequisite of building or inhabiting the land of the free. It would be contradictory for those who would build or inhabit the land of the free to require that all those who would build or inhabit the land of the free hold beliefs if those people did not already freely hold them. But it is not said that these people do not already hold these beliefs. So unless the only or the primary reason why people do hold that common set of basic beliefs that we all hold in America — or that we must hold to belong to America — is the fact that we have to hold them to be American, there is nothing contradictory about claiming that Americans must have a common set of basic beliefs.

Necessary Thoughts and Free Thinkers

There is another sense in which freedom and necessity need not be mutually exclusive. There are some beliefs that we can both freely form, freely grasp, and freely assent to and that we are not free not to hold once we have formed, grasped, or assented to them. It may be that not everyone believes that it is self-evident that Chopin is a great composer. This particular belief is not a necessary belief. But there are a number of beliefs that anyone who holds either that Chopin is a great composer or that Chopin is not a great composer must have in order to hold this belief. The first is that this belief, whatever the belief, is true. That Chopin really is a great composer or that Chopin is really not a great composer. True here is not to be mistaken for absolutely true. I do not mean to suggest that we must believe that our beliefs can in no way be completed or corrected in order for us to believe them. We could hold no beliefs if we thought this. I am claiming that we cannot hold a belief if we do not grasp that that belief corresponds in some significant way to the reality that it describes or explains. Our beliefs are our mental relations to reality. They are the way that we describe, explain, and interact with reality. They refer intrinsically to reality. Beliefs are about things. But to refer to reality, a belief should correspond to it in some significant way, and beliefs are true to the degree to which they correspond to reality. Our beliefs should correspond to reality. It is in intention of believers that their beliefs correspond to reality. We need our beliefs to correspond to reality. The more closely our beliefs correspond to reality, the more easily we can interact with reality, and the more easily we can interact with reality, the fewer problems we will have. False beliefs really do get in our way. We know this by experience. To have believed that a person is trustworthy and to realize that one's belief was mistaken is truly painful. To have believed that a situation warranted a certain way of behaving and to realize that one's belief was mistaken can be truly embarrassing. I am thinking here of situations where we believe that we can speak freely about certain people and end up offending the person with whom we are speaking. We want true beliefs. We need true beliefs.

We must also believe that we are thinkers who are capable of understanding reality and recognizing when beliefs are true in order to hold beliefs. This is especially true if we are to accept or form beliefs by freely thinking about them, by

reflecting upon them. If I believe that Chopin is a great composer because I have reflected on his music and on my reaction
to his music, I also have to believe that I can think. That I can
understand things. That those beliefs that I do form reflect
reality. Naturally there are times when we all question our
ability to think, when we wonder whether we can really formulate coherent believable thoughts or reasons for believing
them. This happens especially when we are tired, distressed,
or have simply spent too much time alone. This is when we
go over and over thoughts and cannot find our way toward
some solution to the problem that we are reflecting on. This
is when we get wrapped up in ourselves, when we cannot trust
what we are thinking, and cannot accept those beliefs that we
do formulate or ponder. But times such as these are precisely
the moments when we suspend our belief, when we do not
accept any of those beliefs that we do form, except perhaps
the belief that we are in no position to accept beliefs, to recognize their validity. But if we do not accept beliefs when we
do not trust ourselves or believe that we are actually capable
of understanding reality and recognizing true beliefs, then we
must trust ourselves and believe that we are actually capable
of understanding reality and recognizing true beliefs when
we do accept beliefs. We must believe that we are capable of
understanding reality and recognizing true beliefs in order to
hold any belief at all. This is especially true for those beliefs
that we form freely.

Again, we must believe that we are free if we are to hold
anything but the most elementary beliefs. Holding a belief
entails understanding that that belief is true. Understanding
this often requires reflection. And reflecting is one of those

acts that is and must be freely chosen. It entails the decision to reflect. But we would not choose to reflect were we not to believe that reflecting is crucial to our holding beliefs. If we believe that choosing to reflect is crucial to our holding beliefs, however, we must believe that we are free. Choosing is the act of a free being. We have all had trouble understanding what we should believe about some things. And what we realize when we are in this sort of predicament is that if we do not think about our beliefs, we will not really understand what beliefs we really have. It does us no good if other people have firm beliefs. The fact that other people have firm beliefs does not give us firm beliefs. Other people cannot understand things for us. Nor does it do us any good to touch the pages of a book, watch a movie, or have a cocktail when it comes to understanding what we really believe about some things. Until we decide to think about the beliefs of which we are not certain, we will not understand where we stand. And no one can force us to decide to think about our beliefs. No one can force us to reflect on or think about anything. People can punish us or threaten to punish us if we do not think. They can say horrible things about us if we do not think. But threats and punishments cannot force us to think. They can make our lives miserable. But miserable lives need not force us to think. If we decide not to think, we will not think, and there is nothing anyone else can do about this. But if we do decide not to think about our beliefs, we cannot really have any beliefs, not informed beliefs at any rate, beliefs with which we are satisfied. We will not understand why we believe what we believe, and consequently we cannot justify our beliefs to ourselves. But in order to decide to reflect upon our beliefs, we have to believe that our reflection, our thought, will lead us to better understand our beliefs. That we will not understand our beliefs unless we decide to think. We have to believe that we are responsible to some degree for our beliefs in order to have beliefs.

To hold many of our beliefs, we must also believe that other human beings are similar to us, that they too believe that beliefs require recognition of the truth, that they too believe that they can recognize the truth, that they too believe that they are free. I do not know whether we would hold any beliefs at all if we did not live in a community of thinkers. What I do know is that we would not have the means to formulate our beliefs if we did not live in a community of thinkers. We would not really know a language if we did not live in a community of thinkers, and without knowing a language we could not really formulate thoughts or beliefs of any sort. I also know that we would not have to reflect about a good many things if we did not live in a community of thinkers. How many times does discussing problems with people make us understand the shortcomings of our beliefs, and hence call us to think about our beliefs? Beliefs, as we understand them, presuppose living in a community, learning from those with whom we live. But learning from those with whom we live entails believing what they say. And we could not believe what other people say unless we believed that they too, like us, or perhaps more than us, would not accept a belief if it were not true. We could not believe what they say unless we believed that they, like us — or perhaps more than us — are capable of understanding and recognizing the truth. One of the great disappointments of life is realizing that one's parents and teachers do not have all of the answers. This is what happens during adolescence. It is what makes adolescence so difficult. Adolescence is the time when we feel that our trust was betrayed, when we realize that those whom we thought could do no wrong can make mistakes. It is when we realize that our parents are not superheroes and that our teachers are only human. But adolescence would not be so painful if we had not believed that our parents and teachers could do no wrong when we were children. It would not be so painful had we not believed that they were far more capable of understanding and recognizing the truth than we are. But adolescence is that painful. It does feel like a massive betrayal. We did believe that our parents and teachers had all of the answers when we were children. We did believe in them and what they taught us. We could not have learned from them if we had not believed in them and what they taught us. Had we not learned from them, we would not have many of the beliefs that we do have now.

There are a number of beliefs that we must all accept if and when we have any beliefs at all. These beliefs enunciate the conditions that make it possible for us to have beliefs. They include such things as the beliefs that we can recognize the truth, that we can think, that we are free, and that other human beings can recognize the truth, think, and are free. These are basic beliefs, beliefs without which we could have no other beliefs.

What these beliefs indicate is both that it is not at all true that there are no basic beliefs to which all free thinkers must assent or that all free thinkers cannot come to hold a common set of basic beliefs. There is a set of basic beliefs that all thinkers must accept. These are the beliefs that all of our nonbasic beliefs presuppose. There is a set of basic beliefs common to all thinkers. But if all thinkers must hold these basic beliefs, all free thinkers must hold these beliefs. And if all free thinkers must hold these beliefs, there must be a set of basic beliefs that all free thinkers share. There must be a common set of basic beliefs that hold for all free thinkers.

Basic Beliefs, Freedom, and America

It is this set of basic beliefs upon which our nation was founded. They are the basic beliefs that enunciate the conditions that make it possible for us to have beliefs. They are the basic beliefs that express the most salient characteristics of being human: "We hold these truths to be self-evident, that all men are created equal, and endowed by the Creator with certain inalienable rights, which include life, liberty, and the pursuit of happiness." They are beliefs the acceptance of which cannot violate our right to free thought, precisely because we must all accept them in order to be able to think. They are beliefs the acceptance of which cannot limit our free thought because our free thought presupposes them. They are the common set of basic beliefs of America.

Our common beliefs determine the limits of our freedom. Whatever we say and do, we cannot deny or contradict these beliefs. To do so would contradict not only what our nation is about, our values, it would more importantly contradict what each of us is. We cannot coherently deny that human beings need to believe that a belief is true in order to accept it. To do so would be to contradict ourselves. We could only claim that human beings do not need to believe that a belief is true in order to accept it, if we believed that that belief is true. But to believe that our belief is true and to claim that people need not believe that their beliefs are true is to contradict ourselves. We cannot coherently deny that human beings need to believe that they are free in order to have anything more than very elementary beliefs, because claims like this one require thought that no one but the thinker can formulate. We cannot coherently deny that thinkers other than ourselves want to hold true beliefs, believe that they are capable of holding true beliefs, and are, like us, free. We learn much of what we know from others and could not do so if we believed that they have the same standards that we do with respect to beliefs.

These points have an important consequence. If our set of common beliefs determine the limits of our freedom of thought, if they are the foundation of our nation, then the foundation of our nation cannot be the exercise of human rights per se. It cannot be grounded in what we can do with our freedom. Our nation is grounded in those conditions that allow us to freely exercise our freedom. We cannot expect what we do or can do with our freedom to be the measure of what we or others can and should do with freedom. This would be to allow anyone to do anything, including things that deprive people of freedom. The measure of what we and others can do with our freedom are those conditions that make it possible for us to be truly free. This holds for our thoughts as well as our actions. We cannot expect what we can think freely to be the measure of what we or others can and should accept. We can easily think things that make it impossible for us to think, things that contradict those conditions that allow us to exercise our right to free thought, things that would make us less free to think. The measure of what we and others can think are those conditions that make it possible for us truly to think. These are our basic beliefs. They are the beliefs that justify human rights. The beliefs that delineate the necessary conditions of human flourishing.

Opinions and the Rights of White Men

We fought a war because our freedom has limits, limits that are not simply the rights of thinkers. The Civil War regarded the limits of freedom: the limits of our right to form our own opinions and to act in accordance with them.

Southern economy was built upon slavery. In the Deep South, cotton was king, and cotton, as we all learned in school, was planted, tended, and harvested by slaves. Slaves were one of the primary sources of revenue for the old South. It is estimated that Virginia and the other old Southern states sold some twenty-five thousand slaves a year to the Deep South. The South's dependence on slavery made slavery very much a part of its understanding of the principles that ground our nation: the rights to "life, liberty, and the pursuit of happiness." Southern culture of the nineteenth century was built upon the presupposition that slavery was a just institution.

As absurd as it seems, in 1864 the Southern Presbyterian Church declared that it was heretical — "unscriptural and fanatic" — to claim that slavery was a sinful institution, since Scripture — both the Old and the New Testaments —

does not explicitly claim that it is.[27] Presbyterians were not the only ones to say this sort of thing. Southern Catholics, Southern Methodists, and Southern Baptists all substantially agreed on this point. Many were the individuals of various religious cloths who donned armor to fight in the war because they were convinced that their cause was holy.

Southerners also held that it was both unconstitutional and undemocratic for people to question the institution of slavery,[28] just as they thought that it was illegal to counter slavery by helping slaves escape and by harboring fugitive slaves. They were, of course, right with regard to the second point, at least. Article 4, section 3, of the Constitution claimed as much, at least prior to the Civil War: "No Person held to the Service or Labour in one State under the Laws thereof, escaping into another, shall in Consequence of any Law or Regulation therein, be discharged from such Service or Labour, but shall be delivered up on Claim of the Party to whom such Service or Labour may be due." Southerners were naturally also convinced that the rights to "life, liberty, and the pursuit of happiness" applied equally to all persons and citizens. They simply added the proviso that these rights were not applicable to blacks, since they were not citizens. The Dred Scott Case went a long way to bolstering their interpretation of this point.

The constitutional rights involved in the case of slavery, in the Southern view, were the rights of plantation owners, whom the Constitution did recognize as persons and citizens, and not the rights of slaves, whom the Constitution did not recognize as persons and citizens. Indeed, it was not uncommon for Southerners to defend their "institution" in the name of the personal freedom and rights of plantation own-ers. Jefferson Davis, for instance, did when he claimed that "abolition is the perfidious interference in the rights of other men." Many people in the South were convinced that their constitutional rights were being violated by Northern aboli-tionists who had halted the emergence of new slave states in the Union, although they did nothing to stop the admission of free states: "It is so that you may have the opportunity of cheating us that you want to limit slave territory within cir-cumscribed bounds. It is so that you may have a majority in the Congress of the United States and convert the govern-ment into an engine of Northern aggrandizement.... And why? Because you want, by an unjust system of legislation, to promote the industry of the North-East States, at the expense of the people of the South and their industry."[29]

At first glance, at least, Southerners were right. It was per-fectly legal to own slaves in the South in the 1860s. Slavery was a constitutionally based right of white men at that time. What is more, there was at that time simply no constitu-tional lever with which to extend those rights, which the Declaration of Independence claims self-evidently to belong to "all men," to all human beings who lived within the United States. Prior to the Thirteenth Amendment, it made no con-stitutional sense to interpret "equality," or the statement "we hold these truths to be self-evident that all men are created equal," as things that necessarily hold for all human beings. Constitutionally speaking, "equality" was not something that was necessarily to be extended to women, let alone to blacks. There was, as such, no constitutional way of backing (or en-forcing) the abolitionist claim that it did necessarily hold for all human beings who lived within the United States. For all of these reasons, it made perfect constitutional sense in the 1860s to claim that abolition is simply the "interference in the rights of other men."

And as this is true, it is also true that, constitutionally speaking, the nineteenth century's growing Northern opposition to the expansion of slavery could be construed as a classic case of discrimination, that is, as a violation of the rights of Southern white men — of their right to practice slavery, of their right to believe that slavery was a just institution, of their right to export what they thought was a just institution to territories other than their own, of their right to have an equal say in the matter of which States should be admitted into the Union, and so on and so forth.

Southerners, in other words, could very well cry that their rights, the rights of slaveholders, that is, were being unconstitutionally violated by Northerners.[30] And those shots fired on Fort Sumter in April 1861 were just the South's way of defending itself against what it perceived as an increasingly aggressive North, which they thought had betrayed everything for which the Union stood. The North had betrayed the ideals of democracy by not allowing Southerners their proper voice in matters of the federal government. It had betrayed the Bill of Rights by not allowing Southerners their own interpretation of the principles of the Union.

The Rights of Other White Men to Their Opinions

The North's perspective on this matter was, of course, radically different from the South's. Slavery had never been a particularly established institution in the North. This is not to say that Northerners had never owned slaves. Abigail Adams's own father owned two slaves. It is also not to say that most Northerners had always been horrified by slavery, but there were those Northerners who were convinced that it was immoral from the very beginning of our nation's history. In 1700, Samuel Sewell spoke out against it in his work *The Selling of Joseph*. In 1761 James Otis, one of the Boston firebrands who was incensed by British taxation, demanded the immediate liberation of all slaves in Massachusetts. John Adams and his wife, Abigail, both spoke loudly against it. Their son John Quincy was even more vehement on the matter than they. Samuel Adams liberated the slave whom he had been given in 1765.[31]

But generally speaking Northerners preferred not to think about slavery or racism. One of Abigail Adams's heroic deeds was that she defended James Price, a young free black boy whom she herself had taught to read and write, when he was asked to withdraw from evening classes at a new school for apprentices. If he did not withdraw, she was told, the other boys from town would themselves withdraw and the school would have to close. Abigail's response was to summon all of the white boys who had remonstrated against Price and ask them whether they thought that theirs was behavior proper to Christians. "Is this the Christian principle of doing unto others as we would have others do unto us?" she asked them. That was the end of the crisis.[32]

And then came the Second Great Awakening, and those Northerners who had hitherto not thought much about slavery discovered that they did not like the institution at all.

There were many reasons for their dislike. One of them, the most basic of them, was what they considered the institution's patent immorality. Northerners were not at all convinced that Jesus' silence on the matter of slavery was to be construed as consent. Quite the contrary; they were convinced that slavery was so obviously evil that it did not take scriptural pronouncements, or divine revelation, to realize that it was. One cannot very well love one's neighbor as oneself by enslaving the neighbor.

Northerners were also convinced that the sinfulness of slavery would spread like a disease and weaken the Union. This, they were increasingly convinced, bordered on blasphemy.[33] After all, the preachers of the Great Revival insisted that the United States was a holy endeavor: "A New Jerusalem, sent down from heaven, Shall grace our happy land," as the poet Phillip Freneau phrased it.[34] There was no doubt in their minds about this. "God," as John Rogers pointed out in one of his New York sermons, "has put all of the blessings of liberty, civil and religious, within our reach, perhaps there was never a nation that had the fair opportunity of becoming the happiest people on earth, that we have now."[35]

But even a budding New Jerusalem can turn foul, especially when people do not follow divine commands. Adam and Eve lost their paradise. And indeed many, like Lyman Beecher (Harriet Beecher Stowe's father) and Emerson warned that America could not become the New Jerusalem if Americans lost sight of their moral and religious identity. Slavery, at least as far as Northerners were concerned, was one of those things that ran afoul of the New Jerusalem, which was to be built on liberty. Liberty and slavery, they thought, are not good bedfellows.

What made this latter point especially poignant were the nation's western territories. The North was as convinced that these had to be "free" territories as the South was that they had to be declared "slave" territories. The North's position derived both from its abhorrence of slavery and from its genuine concern for Northern workmen and their right to the pursuit of happiness: "Extending slavery to the territories would undermine northern liberty because it would destroy the system of free labor.... What saved the northern wage laborer from remaining a hireling for life was the possibility of saving enough to move West and start a farm or a shop of his own. But if slavery spread to the territories, this outlet would be closed."[36]

Northerners, like Southerners, had the constitutional right to question the morality of slavery. The First Amendment gave them that right. They also had the right to act in accordance with their understanding of the "peculiar institution," just as Southerners did in accordance with theirs.

It is also true that they had no constitutional leg to stand on when it came to harboring and aiding runaway slaves. The Constitution made that specific act illegal. But Northerners felt that its illegality did not make it immoral. What is more, with the growth of the abolitionist movement, Northerners began to question the very groundedness of the Southern "right" to own slaves. That specific right, after all, presupposed that "all men" were *not* endowed with the inalienable rights of life, liberty, and the pursuit of happiness, that all men were not created equal. If all men are created equal and endowed with these rights, no man can be enslaved. But the Declaration of Independence does claim that all men are endowed with these inalienable rights. And the Declaration of Independence formulates the principles upon which our nation is founded. If the principles upon which our nation is founded are contrary to slavery, Northerners then found that they could ask, what right can any person in America have to own slaves? And if no one has the right to own slaves, they continued, why should we be called upon to return what no one has the right to own? Why should we believe that the opinions of Southern slave owners are valid?

It was again true that there was no constitutional extension of the principles of the Declaration of Independence to "all men." But the intentions of the Founding Fathers made it clear that they were favorable to this extension. Jefferson, for instance, not only spoke out against slavery, but wrote profusely against it.[37] There was a higher law, as such, which Northerners could invoke to defend their aiding and abetting runaway slaves. And invoke it, they did. Lincoln regularly quoted Jefferson's views on slavery.

Opinions and the Death of the Union

Our nation headed straight for a deadlock. The South argued that it had the constitutional right to its opinions, its "peculiar institution," and the right to export its "peculiar institution." The North argued that it, too, had the right to its opinions and to export them as well, and that in its view the "peculiar institution," Constitution or not, was wrong.

Slavery had split the nation. This was the general consensus in the North: "The policy and aims of slavery, its institutions and civilization, and the character of its people are all at variance with the policy aims, institutions, education, and character of the North. There is an irreconcilable difference in our interests, institutions, and pursuits; in our sentiments and feelings."[38] This was also the consensus of those in the South, or at least those in power in the South. That is why those shots were fired on Fort Sumter.

The Rights of Thinkers, Our Morality, and Our Unity

What the Civil War issues illustrate are the high price of making the rights of thinkers the only means of judging the adequacy of thoughts. That price would have been our *morality,* our *unity,* our *democracy,* and our *freedom.*

Morality was the first obvious price. When push comes to shove, Southerners had as much right to their thoughts as Northerners did to theirs. Had the rights of thinkers been the gauge by which to judge the validity of thoughts as such, we might still have slaves in our country, and have no means to claim that slavery is wrong. For every time anyone claimed that there was something deeply immoral about slavery, Southern slave owners simply could have responded that they had the constitutional right to their own opinion that slavery was not immoral, and let the matter rest at that. Had the rights of thinkers been the gauge for the validity of their thoughts, there would have been no adequate response to their point. And as there would have been no adequate response to slavery, there would have been no adequate response to any other question regarding any other moral issue. If slavery is not wrong, nothing else can be deemed wrong. Slavery is a breach of the inviolability of a human being. If it is not immoral to breach the inviolability of a human being, nothing is immoral.

Unity was the second price of making the rights of thinkers the gauge for the validity of our thoughts. Lincoln pointed out as much: "A house divided against itself cannot stand. I believe this government cannot endure half *slave* and half *free*. I do not expect the Union to be *dissolved*. I do not expect the House to *fall*. But I *do* expect it will cease to be divided. It will become *all* one thing, or *all* the other. Either the *opponents* of slavery will arrest the further spread of it, and place it where the public mind shall rest in the belief that it is in the course of ultimate extinction; or its *advocates* will push it forward, till it shall become alike lawful in *all* the states, *old* as well as *new, North* as well as *South*."[39]

No nation can be united if its people do not have a common understanding of their common goals and principles. If a baseball player were not to understand or accept the goal of his team — to play and win games, let's say — or the rules of the game, he could not be a productive member of his team. How could a player understand what to do on the field during a game, if he did not understand what his team was trying to do? How could he play with the team, if he did not accept the rules of the game or the team's goal, that is, to win a game? Think of what it would be like if a pitcher were convinced that the goal of his team is to play elegantly and to give the other team as many chances to hit the ball as possible, since hitting is an elegant thing and has the added benefit of allow-ing the fielders to make elegant plays. He would throw balls in the middle of the plate all the time and obviously allow many hits. He would clearly put his team in peril every time he stepped on the mound — that is, if the goal of his team were to win. And if his team were to lose, he would not feel responsible for the loss or for the rage of his teammates, since he would not have understood (or accepted) the team's goal to begin with.

Being a team presupposes a common understanding of the goals and principles of that team. And the fact of the matter is that nations are like teams. If every member of a given group of people were to have a different view of the principles and the long-term and short-term goals that the group as a whole should have — of the priorities in life, of the values that cannot be forsaken, and so forth — everyone would end up doing their own thing. There is very little chance that the members of that group would be able to coordinate their efforts at all. They would not, as a result, be able to form a functioning society. The same thing would obviously be true of a group of people divided into different parties with significantly different agendas.

The North and the South had significantly different views of both the aims and principles of our nation. Had the rights of thinkers been the gauge for the validity of thoughts, the North and South could never have come to a consensus with regard to the aims and principles of our nation, and our nation would have been destroyed. Rights of thinkers are things that belong to individuals singly. And things that belong to single individuals are not a common ground of anything. We all have the right to our own views. But my right to my own personal views does not constitute the starting point for any discussion with anyone, let alone the ground for our unity.

The unity of our nation was not all that would have been destroyed had the rights of thinkers been the measure of the validity of our thoughts. For just as a lack of a common understanding of common principles and goals destroys a nation, so too does it destroy any sort of community.[40]

The Rights of Thinkers and Our Democracy

The third price of our making the rights of thinkers the measure of the validity of our thoughts was our democracy. There was a deep contradiction in the opinions of Southern slaveholders. In the interests of their economy, those in power in the South had interpreted those principles upon which our nation is built as things that hold only for a *part* of the American population. This is meant in two main ways. First and most obviously, slave owners did not extend those rights with which we believe all men "self-evidently" to be endowed to *all* men. They left a vast majority of the people altogether out of the picture. By this I do not only mean that they left the slaves out of the picture, which was important enough. Slaves constituted nearly a third of the population of the entire South and more of the population of the Confederate States.[41] Slave owners also cut non–slave owners out of the picture.

Despite the Southern claim to abide by democratic principles, it was the slave owners' agenda that dominated Southern politics. It was the slave owners who dragged the entire South into a long and bloody war over the matter of slavery. And the sad truth is that most white Southerners, 95 percent of them, did not own slaves and could not have profited from the war.[42] This 95 percent of the Southern population was not consulted when the Southern states decided to secede: "In his inaugural, Davis said the Confederacy was born of 'a peaceful appeal to the ballot box.' That was not true. No state held a referendum. It was decided by a total of 854 men in various secession conventions, all of them selected by legislatures, not by the voters. Of these 157 voted against secession. So 697 men, mostly wealthy, decided the destiny of 9 million people, mostly poor."[43] Slave owners were not interested in the rights of others, the rights of whites or blacks. They violated the civil liberties of both. They enslaved the blacks and imposed their war on the whites.

What this indicates is a second and even more important matter. Slave owners were not interested in the welfare of others, neither the welfare the South as a whole nor of the nation as a whole. They were not interested in the common good, one might say. They were interested in their own personal welfare, in the survival of a system that had made them immensely rich, and they expected everyone else to be interested in their personal welfare too. They had created a workforce that ensured their welfare by working for them without wages, and they claimed that it was their civil right to have this workforce.

On both of these counts, Southern slave owners violated the most basic principles of democracy. They violated them both because they were not interested in the welfare of the nation and because they made other people the unwilling means of their welfare. No nation can be a functioning democracy if *all* of its members do not freely accept to be responsible for the welfare of the nation as a *whole*. This is the basic presupposition of a functioning democracy. It is the challenge of a democracy. And it is a challenge to which slave owners did not rise, obviously.

Slave owners also kept others from rising to this challenge. For if it is true that *all* members of a democratic nation must freely accept responsibility for the welfare of the nation, then it must also be true that no nation can be a functioning democracy if all of its members are not *free*. How can individuals freely accept responsibility for their nation if they are told what they must do and what they must not, if none of their choices are free?

There was a deep contradiction in the Southern interpretation of the kind of democracy that the Founding Fathers and revolutionaries tried to build. For all of their love of democracy, slave owners wanted to extend democracy to the few and for the benefit of the few. And since the Constitution sanctioned their understanding of the premise of their view — the legality of the institution of slavery — they believed both that their interpretation was justified and that it was their right to be members of the privileged few.

This led to their most pernicious position: the belief that rights are privileges that absolve people from their duties with respect to others. It is also for this reason that Lincoln claimed that the "house divided against itself" could not stand. Our nation simply could not have survived as a democracy if the view that people are not responsible for the welfare of their nation had survived; it could not have survived if people had been allowed to believe that their rights absolved them of their responsibilities to others.

Had the Southern gentry's rights to its own opinions made its beliefs regarding the goals of our nation acceptable, we could not have continued to be a democracy. Nor could we have been the land of the free. It is because we want to protect our freedom that we are a democracy. If we are not built upon the consent of the governed, our nation cannot be the land of the free.

The Limits of Freedom

It is not by chance that we would have lost our morality, our unity, our democracy, and our freedom had we made the rights of thinkers the only means with which to gauge the validity of our thoughts. Morality, unity, democracy, and freedom are interconnected. Just as we cannot protect our freedom without being a democracy, so too is it true that we cannot be a democracy if we do not have a common understanding of our common principles and goals. It is also true that we cannot have a common understanding of common principles and goals unless something other than the rights of thinkers is used as the standard to measure the validity of our thoughts.

Madison made this point too, and in the same paper in which he spoke out against imposing opinions on people: "The diversity in the faculties of men, from which the rights of property originate, is not less an insuperable obstacle to a uniformity of interests. . . . From the protection of different and unequal faculties of acquiring property, the possession of different degrees and kinds of property immediately results; and from the influence of these on the sentiments and views of the respective proprietors ensues a division of the society into different interests and parties. The latent causes of faction are thus sown in the nature of man; and we see them everywhere brought into different degrees of activity, according to the different circumstances of civil society. A zeal for different opinions concerning religion, concerning government, and many other points, as well as speculation as of practice; an attachment to different leaders ambitiously contending for pre-eminence and power; or to persons of other descriptions whose fortunes have been interesting to the human passions, have, in turn, divided mankind into parties, inflamed them with mutual animosity, and rendered them much more disposed to vex and oppress each other than to co-operate for their common good."[44]

So what should the standard be for the validity of our thoughts? The answer, I am afraid, is that it can only be that one thing that violates no human rights at all — not the rights of the thinker, or the rights of the listeners, not the rights of a community, or the rights of a nation — and that is truth.

The point here was, perhaps, best made by those Puritans whose dream still defines the heart and soul of the American dream. What the Puritans realized is that there is more to building a free society than just ensuring that its civil laws and government are in place through the free and voluntary consent of the people. For that free and voluntary consent need not be of people who understand laws or justice. And if it is not, it cannot produce a free society. The Puritans, who dreamed of building the "City on the Hill" knew it.

Thus, they added a proviso to their definition of the means necessary for forming a society: "Power of Civil rule, by men *orderly chosen*, is God's ordinance," as the very Puritan John Davenport of Connecticut was to say.[45] That is, they held not only that consent must be at the basis of a just government — that the power of civil rule must be "chosen" — but also that that consent must be "orderly," that is, the consent of people who followed and understood God's laws. It is, they thought, only the consent of people who followed God's laws that can ensure that civil laws and civil leaders were just for the "Power of Civil rule . . . is God's ordinance."

The tragedy of the Civil War is that conformity to a morally just standard — God's ordinance — was imposed upon the people of the South through a long and bloody war. For as necessary as it is, at times, imposition is never a good thing. It keeps people from freely accepting the common standard, and only a people who freely accepts and adheres to the truth can have that unity of understanding that allows for a democracy. It is only a people who freely consent to live in accordance with the truth who can be a democracy, and it is democracy that makes us the land of the free.

Five

The Promise of Freedom

Can a nation be founded on freedom? Can a nation truly be grounded in the inalienability of human rights and the inviolability of the human being? I am not asking whether a nation can be a half-hearted imitation of the land of the free, a people who could live freely but abdicate their right to do so by convincing themselves that freedom is nothing more than an inflated form of egoism, or that their voices and views have no place in public affairs. Nor am I asking whether a nation can be just nominally grounded in freedom — a people with a beautiful constitution and sound principles that no one respects. What I am asking is whether a nation can really be built upon freedom, upon the inalienability of human rights, and the inviolability of human beings. I am asking whether an entire people can be bound by these principles, love them, and follow them.

Had we asked this question when our nation was first founded, the response to it would have been twofold. On the one hand, idealists, ideologues, and all manner of enlightened people would have leapt to their feet and cried, "Yes!" and would have proceeded to map out perfect ways of perfecting humankind.

On the other hand, the practical people, the realists, those who know just how difficult it is to make dreams come true, would have been much more cautious. Nations built upon freedom, on the inalienable rights of human beings, they would have claimed, sound like fairy tales, and as wonderful as fairy tales are, fairy tales are just fairy tales. They do not take the hard day-to-day life of a fallen race into consideration. They do not mention the nastier parts of even the best of human lives: the doubts, the fears, the temptations, the greed, the egoism that beset all of humankind. And, these realists would have claimed, it is precisely these day-to-day things that make a democracy so difficult to build. It is these day-to-day considerations that made all attempts to build democracies miserably fail before our country was founded. Democracies are a shared responsibility, they would have pointed out, and it is very difficult for flawed people to put aside their own personal interests to the point of being able to take responsibility for their democracy. Democracies require a people to form freely a common understanding of their common goals, they would have claimed, and the tendency of our fallen race toward egoism is so marked that it is well nigh impossible for an entire people to think objectively of the common goals of their nation. Democracies, they would have concluded, are impossible ideals.

In every part of the world but ours, the idealists and the realists fought each other tooth and nail when it came to building a nation. And in those countries where the idealists won the battle, blood baths devoured all of those people who attempted to express their own opinions about the plans that the idealists had mapped out in order to create the perfect democracy. It is thus that the French Revolution ended, and the Russian Revolution after it. Guillotines chopped away at the heads of tens of thousands of noblemen, clergymen, and other such enemies of the republic when the idealists gained control of France. The Vendée was literally decimated for resisting the ordinances of the *Comité de la Santé Publique* — Committee of Public Safety. Millions upon millions of people died in Russia when the idealists gained control of that country. Poets and composers, thinkers, farmers, children, priests, and countless other people were sent to gulags for crimes as innocent as dancing at the wrong place and time, writing a private poem that criticized Stalin, the leader of the Communist Party, or simply for being too independent. Mandelstam died for having written a poem that was not even published during his lifetime. Salamov was sent to a gulag for being too independent. The horror of their stories is enough to make one's blood freeze.[46]

In those countries where the realists won the battle, democracy was considered to be too much of a risk to be put into practice precisely because it demands so much of the people. Realists opted for more stable forms of government. This is what happened in Germany when the modern German nation was formed from the multitude of German duchies, princedoms, and kingdoms, and in Italy, when the Italian regions became a single state. Both nations became monarchies with very strong aristocratic classes. And as for the people, they had very little to do with the birth of their nations, and very little say with regard to the sort of nation they were to become. Their rights and voices were not really the concern of nation-builders. Lampedusa makes this point with brilliant Italian obliqueness in his masterpiece, *Il Gattopardo*, when he has Don Ciccio Tumeo, the organist of the Mother Church of Donnafugata, a fiefdom of the Sicilian prince Fabrizio Salina, tell his prince that

Donnafugata's plebiscite, which made Salina's lands a part of the kingdom of Italy, could not have been unanimously in favor of deposing the king of Naples, since he had voted against it: "They call them 'alms' today, the generosity of real kings. They call them that so that they do not have to give them themselves. But they were the just compensation of true loyalty. And today if those saintly Kings and beautiful Queens were to look down from Heaven, what would they say? The son of Don Leonardo Tumeo has betrayed us! Thank God the truth is known in Heaven. . . . My no [in the plebiscite] has become a yes."[47] The Italian *Risorgimento* — the war that liberated Italy from foreign domination and unified the various Italian duchies, princedoms, and kingdoms — was a staged affair; it was effected through uncounted votes and the decisions of a very select few. A similar thing could be said of the unification of Germany.

The point is that building the land of the free seems to be an impossible task. When people of good sense looked at our nation as it was being founded, they thought that it would never last. No one had ever attempted to build a republic the size of ours before we did. The British kept troops on our land and snagged sailors off our ships, claiming that once a Briton one was always a Briton, long after the Revolutionary War was over. They were waiting for us to fall apart. Our own Founding Fathers did not expect our Constitution to last. They considered it an experimental constitution.

And yet we proved them all wrong. Ours is the first modern democracy. It is the oldest living modern democracy. It is by far the longest lasting democracy in history, with the exception perhaps of some of the Swiss cantons. It is by far the most successful democracy of history. For all that we complain about our nation, fear for our nation, wish that our nation were a closer approximation to the ideal democracy, we must never forget these things. We may not be the perfect land of the free, but we are the closest approximation to that ideal yet.

What made our country different? How did we avoid the blood baths, the endemic purging, that marked the birth (and death) of other republics? Why did we never even consider the easier route — becoming a monarchy or an institution-alized oligarchy? The answer to this question is threefold. There are three interrelated characteristics of our people and history that made our attempt to become the land of the free vastly different from any other such attempt before or after it: the first is our deeply rooted faith; the second is our love of independence; the third is our practicality.

Faith, Science, and Dreams of Perfect Worlds

Faith is the single-most underestimated element of American culture. In recent times it has been almost completely omitted from our history books.[48] We are taught that America is the embodiment of secular philosophy: the Enlightenment. We are taught that the Founding Fathers envisioned a dividing wall between church and state, and that in their eyes that wall made the state a-theistic.

In a sense, of course, this is true. There is a wall that sepa-rates our state from our churches. We do not have a national religion. We do not make laws with respect to people's beliefs. It is also true that our Founding Fathers were steeped in the Enlightenment.

But there is a deeper sense in which this is not true. Faith is the single-most important aspect of our culture. Faith is the source of our belief in the inviolability of human beings; faith is the source of our belief in the importance of the "consent of the governed"; faith is the source of our belief in equality; faith is the source of that moral standard that has brought us through our nation's worst crises. Faith has been our guiding "light from above," our bedrock, for the last four centuries.

There are many ways to tell the story of the relation between faith and America. Some tell it by analyzing one or more of the many religious revivals that our land has seen and their impact on our culture;[49] some tell it by pointing out how faith was part and parcel of the mentality of one or more of the Founding Fathers;[50] some tell it by showing the close interrelation between faith and democracy in America;[51] some tell it by indicating that the American Revolution was inconceivable without the Great Awakening of the seventeenth century;[52] some tell it by showing how our nation would be inconceivable without Judeo-Christian metaphysics.[53] The point is that faith is everywhere to be seen in our culture. G. K. Chesterton claimed that our country has the soul of a church. Just how much this is true can be seen in our contemporary debates over just what should be taught to our children in school: creationism or evolutionary theory.

People seem to be embarrassed by our faith in our present day and age. Faith, many academics seem to think, is antithetical to reason, and reason is what should guide human life.[54] Reason is scientific; reason's dictates are demonstrable, they claim, and nothing that is not empirically demonstrable should be accepted as the basis for any human endeavor. Their point would seem to be that anything that does not smack of a laboratory, statistical data, or mathematical formulae should not play any part in anyone's life. Since God does not smack of labs, statistics, or math, they argue as such, God should play no part in anyone's life.

Other academics are relativists, and they are not quite sure that words like "acceptable" or "basis" have any real meaning at all. They are sure that there is no meaning at all in any system that claims to have a handle on absolutes. This is their qualm with religion. For if there is anything religious beliefs, especially those religious beliefs that our country claims as its own, do make claims to, it is a Being who is absolute, and knows absolutes. Postmoderns have no more room for this than the modern scientific technologies.

There is nothing particularly original about either of these two positions. Relativism is nearly as old as philosophy itself. Protagoras claimed that "man is the measure of all things" over two thousand years ago. Materialistic empiricism is nearly as old as relativism. Socrates denounced materialism over two thousand years ago. It makes no sense, he claimed, to think that one can explain why I am sitting here by pointing to my bones and sinews. Bones and sinews do not make decisions. "If one said that without bones and sinews and all such things, I should not be able to do what I decided, he would be right, but surely to say that they are the cause of what I do, and not that I have chosen the best course, even though I act with my mind, is to speak very lazily and carelessly."[55]

Nor is there anything particularly sound about the non-scientific claims made by scientists, or those who with them would want to claim that we should not accept any opinion that is not grounded in empirical demonstrations. Similarly, there is nothing particularly sound about the absolute statements made by the relativists. For all that scientists claim that no undemonstrated statement should ever be accepted, they all accept mathematics. And no one has ever demonstrated that mathematics makes valid claims about this world. It is virtually impossible to prove that basic arithmetical statements — like $1+1=2$ — are valid, let alone demonstrate that they can tell us something about the world that surrounds us. Thus, by the very standards of the scientists, empirical demonstrability cannot be the only criterion for accepting statements as true or plausible. As this is so, there is no rational basis, really, for their claim that God does not exist, or that faith is empty.[56] As for the relativists, the problem with their claim that absolute knowledge is impossible is that it invokes absolute knowledge. Relativists claim that absolute knowledge is impossible, yet they all seem to presuppose that it is absolutely true that there is nothing true.

But there is something dangerous about both of these positions. The danger of the latter is that it destroys human communities. We learned this in the Civil War. If there is no standard that all human beings must respect, there can be no such thing as a society unified in its quest for freedom.

The danger of the former position is that it destroys humankind. It is the danger that plagued France and Russia both, and that made their revolutions bloodbaths. The story of this is quickly told. The French Revolution took place in the golden age of modernity — in the age when the great scientific discoveries of Galileo, Harvey, and Newton had given intellectuals a great deal of respect for, and faith in, human reason. It was an age when it seemed possible for the limitless power of the human mind finally to conquer nature, evil, fear, hunger, and human imperfection. It was an age when the one thing to fear, it seemed, was human superstition and systems that were not based upon reason's self-evident premises. For if the human mind could limit itself to deducing systems from self-evident premises, it was thought, it could understand all things and do all things. It was the age when Diderot and d'Alembert designed what they thought would become the final depository of all human knowledge: the encyclopedia.

The intellectuals were convinced that the only way to create a just France was by giving the French a new constitution that was based upon those self-evident premises that human reason could know directly. It so happened that religious beliefs — the tenets of Christianity — were not, in their view, self-evident premises, but the very thing that they loathed the most: superstitions. Therefore they held that the first and worst enemy of a just government was religion. And since they thought that the most just form of government was democratic and based upon the premise that "all men are equal, brothers, and free" — hence their motto *liberté, égalité, fraternité* — they concluded that the first and worst enemy of democracy was religion.

Religion had a second failing in the eyes of the intellectuals: by claiming that humankind can only be redeemed by God — by faith, grace, the sacraments, and whatnot — it denied that humankind was capable of redeeming itself. And this was a crucial failing to the intellectuals who were convinced that human reason is omnipotent, the bearer of the standards of truth and falsehood, and the builder of all perfect systems. Their faith in reason led them to believe that human-kind could be perfected only if people truly put their minds to the task and built a society based upon reason's self-evident principles. This latter fact made them view religion not just as false, but, more important, as an obstacle to humankind's true perfection.[57] We cannot put our mind to the task of perfecting humankind, or redeeming it, if we are convinced that the task cannot be accomplished by mere mortals. And we cannot be convinced that mere mortals can perfect and redeem humankind if we believe in God.[58]

It so happened that the intellectuals managed to gain control of the French government. And that was when the grim side of their project came to light. The French intellectuals set out to do just what modern scientists are attempting to do today: create a perfect world by destroying everything that has to do with anything undemonstrable — religion chiefly — and replacing it with a perfect scientific world. They converted Paris's Cathedral, the Notre-Dame, into a temple for the worship of reason, which they called "the Goddess Reason."

The problem was that they became so busy trying to formulate and enforce their perfect constitution that they forgot all about the very principles that they were trying to uphold: *liberté, égalité, fraternité* — liberty, equality, and brotherhood. Far from treating all human beings as though they had intrinsic value — as beings who were free and equal to them — they *forced* all French citizens to abide by their laws. And far from treating all human beings as brothers or sisters, they *killed* anyone who opposed their ways.

This is not altogether surprising. Once people try to create a perfect society through their science, they set themselves and their ideas up as the standard that others should respect. They and their ideas become the measure of how others should and should not be and behave. By doing so, they treat other human beings as inferior to both themselves and their ideas. This is to lose sight of equality. It is also to lose sight of freedom, of individuals' right to be who they are, to make their own decisions, and to develop their potential as they see fit. In order to build their perfect world, intellectuals must force people to conform to the standards of their rationality.

This points to the deepest problem with the project of the intellectuals: it overlooked human dignity. Those who would create perfect worlds cannot value human beings. There are many reasons for this. The most basic is that human beings are unique individuals. Uniqueness is something with which science cannot deal and consequently which it cannot value. Scientific laws hold for all things equally, and sciences only deal with things insofar as they fall under laws. Uniqueness falls under no law; that is why what is unique is unique. If one wants to uphold sciences over human beings as such, perfect ideas over living persons, one must deny, destroy, and negate everything about those human beings that is unique. This destroys humanity.

The Faith of the Founding Fathers

What saved our country from the excesses of the French Revolution and other similar tragedies was precisely our faith. The Founding Fathers were convinced that democracy was the only just form of government. They were children of the Enlightenment just as the founders of the French Republic were. Some of them seemed to have as much faith in human reason as the French had, and believed in "the sufficiency of human reason for the care of human affairs."[59] Jefferson, it seems, was one of these. But Jefferson, if he was indeed of this opinion, was in the minority.[60] His sympathies for the French Revolution were actually bandied against him when he ran for president: "Should the infidel Jefferson be elected to the Presidency, the *seal of death* is that moment set on our holy religion, our churches will be prostrated and some infamous prostitute, under the title of the Goddess of Reason, will preside in the Sanctuaries now devoted to the worship of the Most High."[61]

On the whole, the Founding Fathers were not at all convinced that human reason was the sufficient condition of a democracy, or any other form of government for that matter. The basic reason for this is that they thought that it is not human reason that creates or establishes the standards to which all human beings must conform. They thought that those standards exist within each human being, as a part of every human being, in virtue of the humanity with which the Creator endowed them all. They etched this in our memories and souls: "We hold these truths to be self-evident, that all men are created equal, and endowed by the Creator with certain inalienable rights, which include life, liberty, and the pursuit of happiness." "Our liberties do not come from charters; for these are only declarations of preexisting rights. They do not depend upon parchment or seals; but come from the King of Kings and the Lord of all the earth."[62]

This belief — that it is not human reason that grants or establishes human rights, but that those rights are part and parcel of the nature with which the Creator endowed humanity — entails that a nation's laws cannot simply be formulations of human reason. Were rights simply human inventions, human ideas, they would only have to abide by the rules of reason. But if these rights are part and parcel of human nature by the will of God, just laws must also respect human nature, just as they must respect both the work of the Creator in this world and the Creator's will, which are the source of that nature. Benjamin Franklin made this clear during the Constitutional Convention: "The longer I live, the more convincing proofs I see of this Truth: that *God governs in the Affairs of Men....* We have been assured, Sir, in the Sacred Writings, that 'except the Lord build the House, they labour in vain that build it.' I firmly believe this; and I also believe, that, without his concurring Aid, we shall succeed in this political Building no better than the Builders of Babel."[63]

And just as they were convinced that it was not human reason that grounded just human laws, so too were they convinced that it was only respect for divine laws that would allow our nation to flourish. They were convinced that it was only if all people — the Constitution writers, the Constitution ratifiers, those in power, and those without power — knew that they were personally responsible to God for what they did and what they failed to do, that our nation could thrive. Washington made this clear in his first Thanksgiving Day Proclamation in 1789, the very first year of his presidency. "It is the duty of all nations to acknowledge the providence of Almighty God, to obey His will, to be grateful for His mercy, to implore His protection and favor," he claimed, and added that we should: "unite in most humbly offering our prayers and supplications to the Great Lord and Ruler of Nations and beseech Him to pardon our transgressions, to enable us all, whether in public or private stations, to perform our several and relative duties properly and punctually, to render our national government a blessing to all people, by constantly being a government of wise, just and constitutional laws, discreetly and faithfully executed and obeyed."[64]

There were several reasons why respect of divine laws was so important to the Founding Fathers. There were practical ones. The Founding Fathers all knew the high risks that were involved in building the land of the free. Being the land of the free, John Adams pointed out, means giving the people "unbounded power": "And the people are extremely addicted to Corruption and Veniality, as well as the Great. — I am not without Apprehensions from this Quarter. But I must submit all my Hopes and Fears to an overruling Providence, in which, unfashionable as the Faith may be, I firmly believe."[65]

The only check for that corruption and veniality, which they knew would certainly destroy the nation, was universal observance of that standard of behavior upon which our nation was built. John Adams made this point too, loudly and clearly: "We have no government armed with power of contending with human passions unbridled by morality and religion. Avarice, ambition, revenge, or gallantry, would break the strongest cords of our Constitution as a whale goes through a net. Our Constitution is made only for a moral and religious people. It is wholly inadequate to the government of any other."[66]

Adams was not alone in this opinion. Congress as a whole claimed much the same thing in the Northwest Ordinance of 1787: "Religion, morality and knowledge, being necessary to good government and the happiness of mankind, Schools and the means of education shall forever be encouraged."[67]

Washington repeated this very point in his Farewell Address of September 19, 1796: "Of all the dispositions and habits which lead to political prosperity, Religion and morality are indispensable supports. In vain would that man claim the tribute of Patriotism, who should labour to subvert these great Pillars of human happiness, these firmest props of the duties of Men and citizens. The mere Politician, equally the pious man ought to respect and to cherish them....Let it simply be asked where is the security for property, for reputation, for life, if the sense of religious obligation *deserts* the oaths in Courts of Justice? And let us with caution indulge the supposition, that morality can be maintained without religion. Whatever may be conceded to the influence of refined education on minds of particular structure, reason and experience both forbid us to expect that National morality can prevail in exclusion of religious principle. 'Tis substantially true, that virtue or morality is a necessary spring of popular government. The rule indeed extends with more or less force to every species of free Government."[68]

There were also religious reasons why respecting God's will was so important. The Founding Fathers were convinced that the root of our nation was a sacred covenant between God and our people.[69] They realized that our unity and victory in the Revolutionary War was not accomplished through our strength alone, that it entailed more than just human work: "The real wonder is that so many difficulties should have been surmounted, and surmounted with a unanimity almost as un-precedented as it must have been unexpected. It is impossible for any man of candor to reflect on this circumstance without partaking of the astonishment. It is impossible for the man of pious reflection not to perceive in it a finger of that Almighty hand which has so frequently and signally extended to our relief in the critical stages of the revolution."[70]

This is why they viewed our independence as a gift from God, a day of deliverance. It was, according to John Adams, to be commemorated by "solemn acts of devotion to God Almighty," for "it is the will of heaven that the two countries should be sundered forever."[71] Throughout the long years of the Revolutionary War, Congress exhorted the nation, the army, to pray: "that he [God] will grant the blessings of peace to all contending nations, freedom to those who are in bondage, and comfort to the afflicted; that he will diffuse useful knowledge, extend the influence of true religion, and give us that peace of mind which the world cannot give: that he will be our shield in the day of battle, our comforter in the hour of death, and our kind parent and merciful judge through time and through eternity."[72] But covenants, they knew, are two-way streets. In order for our nation to receive God's blessing, it had to respect God's will.

Above all there were rational reasons for the Founding Fathers' exhortation to respect divine laws. If those human rights, the intrinsic value of human beings, the defense of which is the first object of government, are to be protected, then that which grounds them and our belief in them must also be protected. But these rights, they were convinced, de-rive from God. What this means is that to abandon faith would be to abandon the very ground of our democracy, the ground of our belief in human equality and the other inalienable human rights: "If [the] empire of superstition and hypocrisy should be overthrown, happy indeed it will be for the world; but if all religion and morality should be over-thrown with it, what advantage will be gained? The doctrine of human equality is founded entirely in the Christian doctrine that we are all children of the same Father, all accountable to Him for our conduct to one another, all equally bound to respect each other's love."[73]

Faith and Reason

The point here is basic to everything that we are. Democracies must be grounded in something that justifies human equality and the rights of men and women to life, liberty, and the pursuit of happiness. Democracies must be grounded in that which confers dignity and inviolability to every individual. So the real question when it comes to democracies is: What grounds human dignity? Why do people have the right to be considered equal to others and the rights to life, to liberty, and the pursuit of happiness?

There are many ways to answer this question. But ultimately it boils down to two responses: either human beings are inviolable by nature, or they are inviolable because someone decides that they are inviolable. That is, people must have the rights to equality, life, liberty, and the pursuit of happiness in virtue of what they are, or because of something other than what they are — something such as the decision of a ruler or set of rulers, a constitution, or even a set of premises that some group of individuals in some café thought self-evident — bestows these rights upon them.

If it is something other than human nature that grants human beings the rights to equality, life, liberty, and the pursuit of happiness, then that which grants these rights must be superior to human beings. Were it not so, it could not have the power to bestow these rights upon people. Thus, if it is a group of intellectuals, a set of ideas thought by intellectuals, or a constitution written by intellectuals that bestows rights upon people, then the intellectuals, their ideas, or their constitution must be superior to human beings.

This is where the problem with most groundings of democracy arises. There is something contradictory and undemocratic about the very idea of claiming that a group of intellectuals, a set of their ideas, or a constitution written by certain individuals can bestow human rights upon human beings. After all, if rights can only be granted by beings who are superior to those to whom they grant rights, then those who grant rights can never grant the right to be equal to themselves, since the beings to whom they grant rights must be inferior to them in order for the right granters to grant them rights. But this is to make some people superior to other people by definition, rather than making them equal. There is, in other words, something contradictory and undemocratic about the whole idea of human beings granting rights to other human beings.

There is also something absurd about it. What would it mean for a person to grant another human being the right to liberty? In order for this incredible gift to have any meaning at all, individuals must not be free before they are given the right to be free. After all, if persons are free by nature, then they cannot but have the right to be free. That right simply cannot be extirpated from any free being, although that being may not be allowed to exercise freedom with impunity. But here is the problem: If we are not free before we are given the right to be free, how does granting that right make us free? To be free means at least to be capable of causing our own acts. So if a person is to grant the right to liberty, that person must at least give beings who are incapable of causing their own acts the capacity to cause their own acts. But how exactly does one do that? To cause individuals to cause their own acts is not to let them cause their own acts. It is to cause them for the individuals. So it would seem to be impossible to bestow the right to be free upon anything, unless one creates it. But this is precisely what law givers, and human beings in general, cannot do.

Therefore, if human beings cannot bestow equality or freedom upon people, and if the equality and freedom of people, among other things, are the conditions of a democracy (that is, the ground upon which democracies are built), then democracies cannot be grounded in human acts. Rather, a democracy must be grounded in what a person *is*, in human nature, and in that which causes that nature to be what it is. It must be grounded in that which can give rights, that which is superior to every human being, that which can create human beings.

This is important because it makes human nature, what is and makes human beings human, and not human reason — that is, what humans are and not what humans think — the ground of a democracy. Namely, it entails that human thought and human laws must conform to reality, to what is, rather than reality, what is, conforming to human thought — the pronouncements of reason. It also makes the ground of democracy superior to every human being: lawgivers and constitution writers, as well as those who have to ratify and accept laws, and thus gives no individual license to violate human rights.

This is precisely the point that our Founding Fathers, as opposed to the many founding fathers of other republics, held most dear. This point made them ground our democracy in the *inalienable* rights of human beings and the laws of the being superior to them, rather than in their own thoughts or opinions. It is what made them invoke human nature and the cause of human nature, God, as the ground of our democracy. This is also what made their democratic experiment coherent.

What saved our country from the excesses of the French Revolution was our faith. What saved us was our belief in God and in the inviolability and sacredness of humankind — that we were made in the image and likeness of God. Faith is the foremost ground of our nation.

Americans and Their Independence

Faith is just one of the characteristics that has made our democracy as successful as it is. The second characteristic that made our democracy work as well as it did is our individual independence, our willingness to take on responsibility not just for ourselves, but also for our nation. We are not a democracy simply because there was a set of brilliant individuals who were born at the right time and at the right place, and who happened to all concur on the fact that democracy was a great thing. We are a democracy because their experiment was successful, because the Founding Fathers managed to write a brilliant Constitution and, above all, because the people of America ratified the Constitution and accepted to live by it.

It was just as important for the people of America to ratify and accept to live by the Constitution as it was for the Founding Fathers to have written their brilliant Constitution. For as true as it is that we could not have been a democracy had we not had the individuals to write our Constitution, to believe in democracy, to hold that "consent of the governed" is the bedrock of proper government and that "the happiness" of the many is the goal of any just government, we certainly could never have become a democracy had we only had brilliant jurists. Constitutions and leaders are not sufficient conditions of a democracy. Democracies also require a people to accept the challenge of being a democracy, that is, accepting to be responsible for their nation and to forward its purposes. No people can be a democracy but the people who are to be a democracy. It was to this challenge that the Founding Fathers called the American people: "It has been frequently remarked that it seems to have been reserved to the people of this country, by their conduct and example, to decide the important question, whether societies of men are really capable or not of establishing good government from reflection and choice, or whether they are forever destined to depend for their political constitutions on accident and force.

If there be any truth in the remark, the crisis at which we are arrived may with propriety be regarded as the era in which that decision is to be made; and a wrong election of the part we shall act may, in this view, deserve to be considered as the general misfortune of mankind."[74] And the American people rose to the challenge. We would not have survived this long as a democracy had we not risen to the task.

Our independence and willingness to take on responsibility for ourselves and others are our inheritance from the settlers. Settling a new continent took a great deal of courage and inventiveness. They lived on a frontier, a strange new world that no one really knew. It was a terrifying world in many ways: a "hideous and desolate wilderness, full of wild beasts and wild men. And what multitude there might be of them they knew not.... If they looked behind them there was the mighty ocean which they had passed, and was now as a main bar and gulf to separate them from all the civil parts of the world," as William Bradford put it in the *History of Plymouth Plantation*.[75] So they all had to think, think quickly, and be ready to act upon their thoughts, or they would have died.

Before they left England they all knew that this was what they would have to do. This is made clear in a London broadsheet called *The Inconveniences that have happened to Some Persons which Have transported Themselves from England to Virginia, without Provisions necessary to sustain Themselves,* which was printed in 1622. The work not only gives a list of those things that no colonizer could live without — axes, tools, and whatnot — it also indicates that colonizing the Americas was not a deed for the weakhearted, or for people who were not willing to depend upon the strength of their limbs and wits for survival.

American Practicality

Our third characteristic is that we are practical people. Perhaps humble, hopeful, or brave are the more appropriate words here. We are people who are not afraid of pursuing an objective, any objective, even though our understanding of that objective may not be perfect. If an objective must be pursued, we will pursue it, even if we are not completely certain that our way of pursuing it is flawless. We are people who prefer not to tarry over things, when it is best to get them done. Once we begin to understand what our objectives are, we figure that it is best to get moving to achieve those objectives because we will not achieve them while we wait. Once we begin to understand our dreams and ideals, we try to realize them immediately because we will not get any closer to realizing our dreams and ideals while we wait. We are also people who are not afraid of pursuing objectives or realizing dreams and ideals, even if there are risks involved in pursuing these objectives and realizing these dreams. We are not afraid of risks. We accept risks as part of life, and proceed to pursue our objectives. We are a hopeful people, a brave people. We are also an honest people. We accept failure as a possibility, just as long as those who fail did their best and bounce up after their failure. In this we are humble. We accept the possibility of failure because we realize that we are human, and to err is human.

At times, our energy and desire to get things done, to pursue our objectives and to realize our dreams, cause us to make mistakes. Big mistakes. How could they not? Our need to do things, to realize our dreams, and to pursue our objectives is so strong that we want to do things, realize our dreams, and pursue our objectives once we begin to understand them, even though our understanding of those dreams and objectives — and of the means to realize those dreams and attain those objectives — may not be perfect. We do not like to wait, unless waiting is imperative. This makes risks and errors a part of our lifestyle. Our practicality is a strength nonetheless, especially when it comes to building a nation.

No one thought that our Constitution was perfect when it was first written. It was a bundle of compromises, composed and discussed point for point by a group of men who came from very different worlds and who had very different interests. Everyone was aware of this: "For when you assemble a number of men to have the advantage of their joint wisdom, you inevitably assemble with those men all their prejudices, their passions, their errors of opinion, their local interests, and their selfish views. From such an assembly can a perfect production be expected?"[76] But this did not stop the Founding Fathers from proposing the Constitution to the people, nor did it stop the people from ratifying the Constitution and enacting it. A union of our states had to be made, and made quickly, if we were to survive as an independent democracy.

We have long forgotten just how urgent it was for us to have that new Constitution. In 1787, our country was facing urgent economic, social, and military problems because of the old constitution. The *Articles of Confederation* had left each state with its own sovereignty. Each had its own army. Each printed its own money. Each still maintained the exclusive right not only to tax its residents, but also to raise tariffs on products made outside their borders. Thirteen sovereign states are an economic, military, and social menace to each other. The history of Europe is an admirable illustration of this fact.

Europeans learn their history in school through their wars. It is a convenient method of learning their history. Once people learn the dates of the most important European battles and treaties, they have a very good framework with which to remember major European events in Europe since the fall of the Roman Empire. For until very recent history, peace in Europe was only an interlude between wars. There is not a single decade in European history (until very recently) during which European countries were not involved in at least one major revolt, war, or battle. War in all of its ugliness has been part and parcel of Europe's history since the fall of Rome.

We risked a similar fate under the *Articles of Confederation* precisely because each state was sovereign under that constitution. States did raise tariffs on each others' products in the early years of our independence, just as they refused to import each others' products. There was a time when the state of New York refused to import Connecticut's wood — it was too expensive, they claimed — and Connecticut retaliated by refusing to import New York chickens. Nor was enmity between states the only risk entailed by having thirteen sovereign states. Each of the states taken singly was politically unstable. There were rebellions within the states — like Shays's rebellion — and these were a grave danger to each of the states. Money was also a problem. There was no common currency in our country while it was bound by the *Articles of Confederation,* and the "continentals" that our central government had issued during the Revolutionary War came to be worth nothing. This impoverished a great many people. The economic and political instability of the states were linked. Alexander Hamilton claimed as much. "If Shays had not been a *desperate debtor,*" he pointed out "it is much to be doubted whether Massachusetts would have been plunged into a civil war."[77]

It was clear to everyone that our country had to change in order to deal with these matters. The Constitutional Convention was called for May 1787. The men involved in it produced a new constitution with breathtaking speed. They managed to produce a Constitution in five months. It was not a perfect Constitution. It had at least one serious flaw: It did not respect the universal rights of *all* human beings. Women, blacks, and Native Americans were not fairly treated by it. Not even the Bill of Rights, which was immediately added to it, rectified this flaw. But here is the problem: should we have waited, taken time to produce yet another constitution, a more perfect constitution? If one were to look at the matter by concentrating on the principles at stake, it would have made perfect sense to wait and write a better constitution. Basic flaws have long-term effects. Our history has taught us as much. But if one were to look at the matter by concentrating on the risks involved in writing a more perfect constitution — not having it ratified by all of the states and not forming a union at all — it did not make sense to postpone a stronger union of the states. Writing a stronger constitution would have put all of the states in danger.

It is with matters such as these that our practicality sets in. There was simply no way to make a better constitution at that time. A better constitution, one that did respect the rights of all human beings, would simply not have been accepted by all states in 1787. So the Constitution writers had to make a choice: accept the Constitution as it was or forgo the union until a more perfect constitution could be written. They chose the former despite the fact that they knew full well that it could cause a civil war. They hoped that the great divide between the states, slavery, would die out on its own.

So it is with all of our history. We did not have a blueprint with which to build this nation of ours. We did not know how to build nations before we started. Our Founding Fathers knew that they wanted to build a land of freedom. They knew that they did not know what building a land of freedom entailed. They knew that there were risks involved in pursuing the dream of freedom. They knew that all democracies that preceded ours had failed miserably.[78] They knew that no one had ever attempted to build a democracy for a nation as large as ours.[79] They also knew that freedom is something worth pursuing, and that there is no way to learn how to build a nation on freedom without trying to do so. So they figured that we would learn how to build a nation as we went along, through our mistakes if necessary. The dream was worth the price: "Hearken not to the voice which petulantly tells you that the form of government recommended for you [American people] is a novelty in the political world; that it has never yet had a place in the theories of the wildest projectors; that it rashly attempts what is impossible to accomplish. No, my countrymen, shut your ears against the poison which it conveys; the kindred blood which flows in the veins of American citizens, the mingled blood which they have shed in defense of their sacred rights, consecrate their Union and excite horror at the idea of their becoming aliens, rivals, enemies.... But why is the experiment of an extended republic to be rejected merely because it may comprise what is new? Is it not the glory of the people of America that, whilst they have paid decent regard to the opinions of former times and other nations, they have not suffered a blind veneration for antiquity, for custom, or for names, to overrule the suggestions of their own good sense?... To this manly spirit posterity will be indebted for the possession, and the world for the example, of the numerous innovations displayed on the American theater in favor of private rights and public happiness."[80] "How few of the human race have ever had an opportunity of choosing a system of government for themselves and their children? How few have ever had anything more of choice in government than in the climate?"[81]

Risks and mistakes are the cost of pursuing freedom. They are the cost of being imperfect. This is also where our practicality is so important. Despite their dreams, their hope, their courage, and their belief in themselves and those principles they pursued, the Founding Fathers knew that we would not and could not build a perfect world. "Amidst all their exultations, Americans and Frenchmen should remember that the perfectibility of man is only human and terrestrial perfectibility. Cold will still freeze, and fire will never cease to burn; disease and vice will continue to disorder, and death to terrify mankind."[82]

And they did make mistakes. Disease and vice did bring disorder, just as the cold froze and fires burned. We did not really know what equality, liberty, or the pursuit of happiness meant when we started off on this adventure of ours. For that matter, we still do not have a clear idea of what these things mean. We are still making mistakes. But this does not mean that our adventure should not be lived, that our dream should not be pursued, or that there is something wrong with our need to build the land of the free. The American dream is about humanity, allowing people to grow freely, to pursue their happiness. There is nothing wrong with this dream. It is the most noble of dreams. It means that we have to learn to accept the fact that we can make mistakes, live with our mistakes, and get back up after we have made them. It means that we must accept the fact that pursuing ideals is a risky endeavor.

It means that we have to learn more fully to appreciate our principles and live in accordance with them if we are to make our ideals a reality. It also means that we can only make our nation a closer approximation of the American dream by following in those bold footsteps of our Founding Fathers. There is only one way to learn to understand our principles and live in accordance with them, and that is to continue that adventure started all of those years ago, with the hope, the joy, the energy, and the perseverance of our Founding Fathers.

What It Takes to Be Free

We have been given a beautiful legacy, the stuff of which dreams are made. We have been born in a nation that, as flawed as it is, respects what we are. We have been born in a nation that views us, the people, as its reason for being. Three things have kept our legacy alive: our faith, our independence, and our practicality. Our faith has mapped out the limits of our freedom. Our independence has made us responsible for our freedom. Our practicality has given us the courage to attempt to become the land of the free.

We are not the perfect land of the free. I am not sure that we ever will be the perfect land of the free, or that we should even think that it is possible for us to build the perfect land of the free. What I do know is that we cannot become the land of the free without understanding what freedom is and how it can be our collective goal.

I began this book claiming that, from the philosophical point of view, there are two basic conditions to building the land of the free. The first is that those who would build and inhabit the land of the free must be convinced that freedom is the primary value, something of intrinsic worth that should be loved and pursued over and above other values, other things of intrinsic worth. The second is that freedom must be pursuable not just by individuals singly, but by a nation as a whole, the battle cry not just of single people who want individually to affirm their rights, but of a nation as a whole. Both of these conditions are difficult to meet. Freedom presupposes things of value: human beings, life, and rationality. And that which presupposes values cannot be a primary value in any absolute sense. Thus, it is almost absurd to claim that freedom is a primary value in any basic sense. Freedom also seems to be incompatible with nationhood, because nationhood requires laws and governments, and both laws and governments seem to limit freedom. It would seem to be contradictory to claim that a nation can be founded on that which it limits. The point is that our nation is built on a set of paradoxes.

These paradoxes have a limited number of solutions. There is really only one sense in which freedom can be thought of as a primary value. That sense has to do with human development. Freedom is a prerequisite of true human growth, of all individuals developing their capacities and striving to be what they can be. Outside the context of individual development, the claim that freedom is a primary value is meaningless. What this means is that human growth, the goals of human life — that is, that which gives meaning to the claim that freedom is a primary value — must set the limits of our freedom. In order to be the land of the free, we have to respect both everything it is to be human — human life, human rationality, human dignity — and that which makes human beings sacred and inviolable. This is why our faith is of utmost importance to our nation. It is the Creator who endows us with our inalienable rights. Our Founding Fathers claimed as much.

There is also only one way for a nation to preserve its citizens' freedom: to make the consent of the governed the source of the government's power. Making the consent of the governed the source of the government's power necessarily makes the citizens of the land of the free responsible for their nation. The power of the nation lies in their consent. People must be independent in order for their nation to be the land of the free. They must be willing to take responsibility for their nation. But grounding a nation in consent also makes the attempt to be built upon freedom a tremendous risk. People can consent to the most atrocious things, damaging themselves and harming others. Consent must, as such, be informed. It must also have limits. There must be some things to which those who would build and inhabit the land of the free cannot ever consent. These limits are dictated by the very reason why freedom is the primary value of our nation, why we protect freedom in the first place. The limits of our freedom are dictated by the sacredness and inviolability of human beings.

The American Legacy

America is a wonder. There has never been a nation quite like ours and there probably never will be another. We truly are the envy, the *Wunderkind*, of the world. We are also one of the most misunderstood nations in the world. Understanding nations in general is not an easy thing. I lived in Italy for years and am not really sure I understand Italian politics, or what Italy is really about. Italians have a strange way of eluding classification. Italians themselves admit that they do not understand Italy. Last summer I was walking downtown Padova, the university city, with a colleague who asked me if I thought that Italians dressed well. The standard response to her question is clearly "Yes." Italians have exported style to the world. Prada, Gucci, Versace, Armani, Valentino, Pininfarina, and Giuggiaro are some of the finest designers in the world. But when I looked around and saw what people were wearing that summer day, I had to say, "No." The Italians I saw walking down the street last summer were not well dressed. They all looked like they were wearing a shabby uniform: shirts with numbers on them and jeans with rips and tears. My colleague looked up stunned and asked, "Ma come?" ("What?") "Look around you," I said. Her response was stunning. "You're right," she agreed. "I no longer understand my country." And she continued by pointing out what Italians do not understand about Italy, most significantly the fact that their nation has the lowest birth rate in the world. I have heard Germans say the same thing about Germany, and I too could say the same thing about Germany even though I lived there for years too. Nations are complex realities.

Our nation is more misunderstood than many. Most Europeans I have met try to understand America through the parameters of their culture and history. If they are very well educated, they apply to our country those complex political theories that they developed in order to understand European history. In so doing, they fall radically short of understanding our nation without realizing that they do. This brand of misunderstanding is to be found in our country too. Many Americans want to apply European political theory and critical theory to our country. By so doing they miss much of what our country is about: the diverseness, the uniqueness, of our nation.

In most cases misunderstanding a nation does not have dire consequences. Italians may not quite understand their politics or their nation, but they seem to get along quite well without it. They have practiced the art of survival for millennia. They have seen the rise and fall of kingdoms, republics, and empires. They have lived under foreign domination, through wars, famines, and dictatorships. So they shrug their shoulders when they realize that they do not understand quite what is going on in their country, and say something along the lines of, "Cosa vuoi?" — "What do you expect?" — or "Si stava meglio quando si stava peggio" — "We were better off when we were worse off." Italians also do not expect people from other countries to understand them. The same thing could be said of Germany. But we are different. Not knowing what we are about does have dire consequences. This is the price of being a young and enormously powerful nation. It is the price of wanting to be the land of the free.

Notes

1. Why Freedom?

1. The phrase is Michael Sandel's. Michael J. Sandel, *Democracy and Its Discontent: America in Search of a Public Philosophy* (Cambridge, Mass.: Belknap Press of Harvard University Press, 1996).

2. See David McCullough, *John Adams* (New York: Simon and Schuster, 2001), 395.

3. McCullough, *John Adams,* 104. Jefferson was also aware of the problem. He complained that slavery violates "the most sacred rights of life and liberty" in the paragraph of the Declaration of Independence that was deleted from the final version of the text. See David Colbert, *Eyewitness to America* (New York: Vintage, 1998), 95.

4. During the debates of the Constitutional Convention, James Madison claimed that the states are "divided into different interests not by their difference of size, but principally from their having and not having slaves." The Constitution did not cure this division. It could only have done so had it made a clear pronouncement for or against slavery. But it did neither, allowing the slavery issue to continue to divide the states. And divide them it did. The first Congressional debates regarding slavery took place in February 1790 and demonstrated that if there was anything clear regarding the slavery issue, it was that the North and South had "competing and incompatible presumptions about slavery in the American republic." The North generally believed that slavery was a dying reality. The South did not. For a discussion of this issue see, Joseph J. Ellis, *Founding Brothers: The Revolutionary Generation* (New York: Vintage Books, 2000), 81–119.

5. Thomas Jefferson quoted in Ellis, 99. See Thomas Jefferson, *Notes on the State of Virginia,* Query XIV (Chapel Hill: University of North Carolina Press, 1955), 130.

6. Our isolationism dates to our first presidents. John Adams contended that the United States should not become involved in Europe's affairs even before the end of the Revolutionary war. In a letter to Congress dated April 18, 1778, he exhorted: "Let us treat them [European powers] with gratitude, but with dignity. Let us remember what is due to ourselves

and our posterity as well as to them. Let us above all avoid as much as possible entangling ourselves with their wars and politics.... America has been the sport of European wars and politics long enough" (McCullough, *John Adams*, p. 235). George Washington expressed his position on this matter, which was identical to Adams's, in his Farewell Address. George Washington, *Farewell Address* (New York: Want Publishers, 1986).

7. This point was not a new one in our country. It first emerged at the end of the nineteenth century after our annexation of the Philippines. There were ferocious debates in Congress on this matter in 1902, during which Senator George F. Hoar claimed, "If a strong people try to govern a weak one against its will, the home government will get despotic too. You cannot maintain despotism in Asia and a republic in America. If you try to deprive even a savage or a barbarian of his just rights you can never do it without becoming a savage or a barbarian yourself." George F. Hoar, in *In Our Own Words: Extraordinary Speeches of the American Century*, ed. Robert Toricelli and Andrew Carroll (New York: Kodansha America, 1999), 6.

8. John Jay, *The Federalist Papers*, ed. Clinton Rossiter (New York: Mentor, 1961), 2, 5.

2. Why We Are Not a Theocracy

9. For a brief history of Islam, see Steven Emerson, *American Jihad: The Terrorists Living among Us* (New York: Free Press, 2002), 221–31. The definition of *jihad* is his.

10. The fundamentalist Islamic threat to basic human rights must not be underestimated. Many fundamentalist Islamic nations simply refuse to acknowledge those rights — Saudi Arabia has as yet to sign the Universal Bill of Rights promulgated by the U.N. in 1948 — and many openly refuse to abide by them. Forced conversions to Islam are unfortunately the order of the day in many parts of the world today, as are massacres of Christians. See Antonio Socci, *I Nuovi Martiri: Indagine sulla Intolleranza Anticristiana nel Nuovo Secolo del Martirio* (Casale Monferrato, Italy: Piemme, 2002); Paul Marshall and Lela Gilbert, *Their Blood Cries Out: The Untold Story of Persecution against Christians in the Modern World* (Dallas: Word Publishing, 1997); Robert Royal, *The Catholic Martyrs of the Twentieth Century: A Comprehensive World History* (New York: Crossroad, 2000). I do not mean to suggest that all of Islam is a threat, but that fundamentalist Islam is.

11. Paul Johnson, *A History of the American People* (New York: Harper-Collins, 1997), 82.

12. Thomas Aquinas, *Summa Contra Gentiles*, ed. — James F. Anderson (Notre Dame, Ind.: University of Notre Dame Press, 1956), II, 4 §1, 34⁻35.

13. Increase Mather, quoted in Johnson, *A History of the American People*, 67. Emphasis in original.

14. This is contrary to the image we commonly have of Virginia, which was colonized not by religious dissidents, but by businessmen. Nonetheless, as James H. Hutson indicates, "Although Virginia, during its first two decades might not have looked like the New England settlements, it certainly sounded like them, for most of the ministers who came to the colony during its early years, whose views can be ascertained, were Puritans.... Like their brethren in New England they shared the view, common throughout Europe, that the state must impose one true religion in its jurisdiction. Accordingly, the Virginia House of Burgesses in 1632 passed a law requiring that there be a "uniformitie throughout this colony both in substance and circumstance to the cannons and constitutions of the Church of England." James H. Hutson, *Religion and the Founding of the American Republic* (Washington, D.C.: Library of Congress, 1998), 18.

3. The Responsibility of Freedom

15. I do not mean to imply that the justice system advocates anarchy. What I mean is that many of the Supreme Court's recent pronouncements indicate that they take freedom simply to be the capacity to make choices, and that this position must interpret any interference in people's capacity to make choices as limiting their freedom. In accordance with this view, the Supreme Court has increasingly advocated a very strong noninterference policy in people's choices, especially those concerning values and ends. See on this point, Michael Sandel, *America in Search of a Public Philosophy* (Cambridge, Mass.: Belknap Press of Harvard University Press, 1996). The entire book deals with this issue. See also Michael J. Sandel, *Liberalism and the Limits of Justice* (Cambridge: Cambridge University Press, 1998).

16. Alexander Hamilton, *Federalist Papers*, ed. Clinton Rossiter (New York: Mentor, 1961), 22, 120. Emphasis in the original.

17. John Adams, Preamble to the Constitution of the Commonwealth of Massachusetts, quoted in David McCullough, *John Adams* (New York: Simon and Schuster, 2001), 221.

18. There are many very good books on this point. See, for instance, Michael Novak, *On Two Wings: Humble Faith and Common Sense at the*

American Founding (San Francisco: Encounter Books, 2002); James H. Hutson, *Religion and the Founding of the American Republic* (Washington: Library of Congress, 1998); Nathan O. Hatch, *The Democratization of American Christianity* (New Haven: Yale University Press, 1989).

19. Paul Johnson, *A History of the American People* (New York: Harper-Collins, 1997), 61.

20. Ibid., 105.

21. Pierre Manent, *An Intellectual History of Liberalism* (Princeton, N.J.: Princeton University Press, 1995), 5.

4. The Limits of Freedom

22. *Planned Parenthood of Southeastern Pennsylvania v. Casey*, 505 U.S. 833 (1992.

23. James Madison, *Federalist Papers*, ed. Clinton Rossiter (New York: Mentor, 1961), 10, 46.

24. Alexander Hamilton, *Federalist Papers*, 1, 2.

25. See, for instance, Deborah Tannen, *You Just Don't Understand: Women and Men in Conversation* (New York: Ballantine, 1991).

26. Their claim is that "Society is best arranged when it is governed by principles that do not presuppose any particular conception of the good, for any other arrangement would fail to respect persons as beings capable of choice; it would treat them as object rather than subjects, as means rather than ends in themselves." Michael Sandel, *Liberalism and the Limits of Justice* (Cambridge: Cambridge University Press, 1998), 9. This is not Sandel's position; it is the one he argues against.

27. See Paul Johnson, *A History of the American People* (New York: HarperCollins, 1997), 470.

28. The first violently pro-slavery government in Kansas declared that it was illegal to question the legality of slavery. Kansas was just repeating the 1790 resolution in Congress that claimed that Congress had "no authority to interfere in the emancipation of slaves, or in the treatment of them within any of the States," a resolution that had Daniel Webster claim in 1833 that he had no authority as a congressman to deal with the matter of slavery. See Joseph J. Ellis, *Founding Brothers: The Revolutionary Generation* (New York: Vintage Books, 2000), 118.

29. Jefferson Davis, quoted in Johnson, *History of the American People*, 434.

30. John Calhoun used this very argument to defend the introduction of slavery into newly acquired American territories. He claimed that these newly acquired territories belonged to all American states — the "states united" as opposed to the United States — and therefore that residents of every state had the right to live according to their customs on these territories. Thus, since slavery was the custom of the South, slavery should be admitted in new American territories. This piece of reasoning was contrary to both custom and prior congressional decisions. The Northwest Ordinance of 1787 prohibited slavery in the Northwest, and in 1820 Congress prohibited slavery north of the 36.30 parallel. Calhoun thus declared these decisions to be unconstitutional.

31. See David McCullough, *John Adams* (New York: Simon and Schuster, 2001), 133.

32. See ibid., 480. Abigail Adams was an incredible woman. Not only did she recognize that there was an inherent contradiction in fighting for freedom and owning slaves, she was also deeply concerned with the contradiction inherent in fighting for freedom and giving women none. See Lynne Withey, *Dearest Friend* (New York: Touchstone, 2002).

33. This was something on which Alexis de Tocqueville also commented: "There is no country in the world in which the Christian religion retains a greater hold over the souls of men than in America.... Religion is the foremost of the institutions of the country" (A. de Tocqueville, *Democracy in America*, ed. P. Bradley [New York, 1948], 303–4).

34. Phillip M. Freneau was considered our nation's Revolutionary poet. He was James Madison's roommate at Princeton. For his poems, see Phillip M. Freneau, *Poems* (New York: Macmillan, 1968).

35. John Rogers, quoted in Michael Levy, "Messianismo del Popolo Americano dalle Origini ad Abraham Lincoln, in *Popoli Messianici*, ed. L. Sartori (Bologna: Centro Editoriale Devoniano, 1986), 134.

36. Michael Sandel, *America in Search of a Public Philosophy* (Cambridge, Mass.: Belknap Press of Harvard University Press, 1996), 179.

37. Jefferson's speaking out against slavery is, of course, one of those mysteries of our nation. There is no doubt that a part of Jefferson loathed slavery. He made this clear in that paragraph of the Declaration of Independence that was deleted from the text: "He [King George] has waged cruel war against human nature itself, violating its most sacred rights of life and liberty in the persons of a distant people who never offended him,

captivating and carrying them into slavery in another hemisphere, or to incur miserable death in their transportation here. This piratical warfare, the opprobrium of Infidel powers, is the warfare of the Christian King of Great Britain. Determined to keep open a market where men should be bought and sold, he has prostituted his [veto] for suppressing every legislative attempt to prohibit or to retrain this execrable commerce. And that this assemblage of horrors might want no fact of distinguished [caprice], he is now exciting those very people to rise in arms among us, and to purchase that liberty of which he has deprived them, by murdering the people on whom he has also obtruded them, thus paying off former crimes committed against the liberties of one people, with crimes which he urges them to commit against the lives of another." See David Colbert, *Eyewitness to America* (New York: Vintage, 1998), 95. It is also true that Jefferson never freed his slaves and spoke with fear about freeing them, most notably in his *Notes on the State of Virginia.*

38. Theodore Sedgwick, in Michael J. Sandel, *Democracy and Its Discontent: America in Search of a Public Philosophy* (Cambridge, Mass.: Belknap Press of Harvard University Press, 1996), 180.

39. Abraham Lincoln, quoted in Johnson, *A History of the American People,* 443. Emphasis Lincoln's.

40. This became obvious in the Civil War. It is one of the reasons why the South lost the war. The Confederacy was simply not able to become a unity of southern states. The states were not even able to make a single unified army: "Each state raised its own forces, and decided when and where they were to be used and who commanded them. To many of their leaders, the rights of their state were more important than the Confederacy itself. Men from one state would not serve under a general from another. Senior commanders with troops from various states had to negotiate with state governments to get more men." Paul Johnson, *A History of the American People,* 465.

41. According to the 1860 census, the eleven Confederate States had a population of 5,449,467 whites and 3,521,111 slaves. The population of the entire South was 8,099,000 whites and 3,953,580 slaves.

42. According to the 1860 census, there were 8,099,000 whites in the South and only 384,000 slave owners. Of the 384,000 slaveholders, 10,781 owned between 50 and 100 slaves; 1,733 owned 100 or more slaves.

43. Johnson, *A History of the American People,* 458.

44. James Madison, *Federalist Papers*, 10, 47.

45. Johnson, *A History of the American People*, 67.

5. The Promise of Freedom

46. I am thinking here of Lev Razgon's recollections of life in a gulag. Their horror is unspeakable. Lev Emmanuilovich Razgon, *True Stories*, trans. John Crowfoot (Dana Point, Calif.: Ardis Publishers, 1997).

47. Giuseppe Tomasi di Lampedusa, *Il Gattopardo* (Milan: Feltrinelli, 1993), 111.

48. Wilfred M. McClay makes this point: "Aside from a handful of moments in American history, notably the founding of New England, where mention of the religious dimension is unavoidable, precious little in the story of American history that survives in our standard textbooks even hints at the strong and abiding religiosity of the American people. It is not clear whether this fact reflects a commitment to philosophical secularism, among the overwhelming majority of academic historians. But it does indicate an enormous gap between such historians and the American people." Wilfred M. McClay, *A Student's Guide to U.S. History* (Wilmington, Del.: ISI Books, 2000), 74–75.

49. One of these people is George M. Marsden. See his *Fundamentalism and American Culture: The Shaping of Twentieth-Century Evangelicalism 1870–1925* (Oxford: Oxford University Press, 1980).

50. Michael Novak, for instance, does this in his *On Two Wings: Humble Faith and Common Sense at the American Founding* (San Francisco: Encounter Books, 2002), but so too does David McCullough in his biography of John Adams.

51. See Nathan O. Hatch, *The Democratization of American Christianity* (New Haven/London: Yale University Press, 1989); James H. Hutson, *Religion and the Founding of the American Republic* (Washington, D.C.: Library of Congress, 1998).

52. See, for instance, Paul Johnson, *A History of the American People* (New York: HarperCollins, 1997), 108–17.

53. Novak, *On Two Wings*, 5.

54. A good example of this can be seen in Quentin Skinner's review of Charles Taylor's book *The Sources of Self: The Making of the Modern Identity*, in which the author claims that "Theism must certainly be false.... It must be grossly irrational to believe otherwise. To say, however, that a belief is grossly irrational is to say that anyone who continues to affirm it must be

suffering from some serious form of psychological blockage or self-deceit."
Skinner in Paul Marshall and Lela Gilbert, *Their Blood Cries Out: The Untold Story of Persecution against Christians in the Modern World* (Dallas: Word Publishing, 1997), 6. Quentin Skinner, "Who Are We? Ambiguities of the Modern Self," *Inquiry* 34 (1991): 148.

55. Plato, *Phaedo*, trans. G. M. A. Grube (Indianapolis: Hackett, 1981), 99 2–5, 137.

56. Thomas Nagel actually admits this in his book *The Last Word:* "I am talking about something much deeper — namely, fear of religion itself. I speak from experience, being strongly subject to this fear myself: I want atheism to be true and am made uneasy by the fact that some of the most intelligent and well-informed people I know are religious believers. It isn't just that I don't want to believe in God and, naturally, hope that I'm right in my belief. It's that I hope there is no God! I don't want there to be a God; I don't want the universe to be like that." Thomas Nagel, *The Last Word* (New York: Oxford University Press, 1997), 130.

57. See, on this point, Pierre Manent, *An Intellectual History of Liberalism* (Princeton, N.J.: Princeton University Press, 1995), xvii: "It is widely believed that the originality of European political history stems from Christianity, and that the development of modern politics can be described as a process of 'secularization.' What are liberty and equality, after all, if not 'biblical values' shaping civic life? The thesis was born and acquired its credence just after the French Revolution. . . . In any case the principles of the new politics — the rights of man and citizen, freedom of conscience, sovereignty of the people — had been forged during the two previous centuries in a bitter fight against Christianity, and particularly against the Catholic Church."

58. What is most amazing is that the premises of the French Revolution appealed to intellectuals throughout the European continent. To Germans like Hegel and Schelling, who planted a tree in honor of the French Revolution, to Swiss intellectuals like Constant, to English intellectuals like Richard Price, the events of Paris became a model of future nation building. They were ready to accept not only that a democracy could only be built upon self-evident principles and that the principles of Christianity were not self-evident, but, more important, that humankind itself was capable of perfecting itself, of building the perfect democracy, if it followed the precepts of reason. Consequently they held that the religious belief that

held that humankind could only be perfected by God made it the enemy of democracy. All of these things were taken up most significantly by Marx, who coined that catchphrase "religion is the opium of the people."

59. Jefferson wrote this in the *Gazette of the United States* upon his return to Virginia from France, which he left in 1789 after the beginning of the French Revolution, but before the terror.

60. Jefferson's opinion on this matter is not altogether clear. For as often as he seemed to claim that human reason alone was "sufficient for the care of human affairs," he also asked: "Can the liberties of a nation be thought secure when we have removed their only firm basis, a conviction in the minds of the people that these liberties are the gift of God? That they are not violated but with his wrath?" Thomas Jefferson, *Notes on the State of Virginia* (New York: Penguin USA, 1998), Query XVIII.

61. *New England Paladin*, quoted in Johnson, *A History of the American People*, 206–7.

62. John Dickson, chairman of the Committee for the Declaration of Independence, quoted in Novak, *On Two Wings*, 95.

63. Benjamin Franklin, quoted in Hutson, *Religion and the Founding of the American Republic*, 76.

64. J. D. Richardson, ed., *Compilation of the Messages and Papers of the Presidents 1789–1797*, 10 vols. (New York: Johnson Reprint Corp., 1969), 1, 64.

65. John Adams, letter to Abigail Adams, July 3, 1776, in *Letters of a Nation: A Collection of Extraordinary American Letters*, ed. Andrew Carroll (New York: Kodansha International, 1997), 63–65.

66. John Adams, "To the Officers of the First Brigade of the Third Division of the Militia of Massachusetts," October 11, 1798, quoted by Michael Novak, "The Influence of Judaism and Christianity," in J. H. Hutson, *Religion and the New Republic* (New York: Rowman & Littlefield, 2000), 177.

67. See H. S. Commager, *Documents of American History* (New York: Appleton-Century-Crofts, 1968), 131. See also R. M. Taylor, ed., *Northwest Ordinance 1789: A Bicentennial Handbook* (Indianapolis: Indiana Historical Society, 1981).

68. George Washington, *Farewell Address* (New York: Want Publishers, 1986).

69. See on this point Hutson, *Religion and the Founding of the American Republic*, 52–58; Novak, *On Two Wings*, 5–24.

70. James Madison, *Federalist Papers*, ed. Clinton Rossiter (New York: Mentor, 1961), 37, 199.

71. John Adams, in David McCullough, *John Adams* (New York: Simon and Schuster, 2001), 130.

72. John Jay, Proclamation of Congress, March 20, 1779, as quoted by Hutson, *Religion and the Founding of the American Republic*, 54. See also Worthington C. Ford and Gaillard Hunt, eds., *Journals of the Continental Congress, 1774–1789*, 34 vols. (Washington, D.C.: Library of Congress, 1904–1937), 4, 209.

73. McCullough, *John Adams*, 619.

74. Alexander Hamilton, *Federalist Papers*, 1, 1.

75. William Bradford, *History of Plymouth Plantation*, in *Colonial American Writing*, ed. R. H. Pearce (New York: Holt-Rinehart-Winston, 1956), 33.

76. Benjamin Franklin's address to the Constitutional Convention on the day of its signing, in David Colbert, *Eyewitness to America* (New York: Vintage, 1998), 116.

77. Alexander Hamilton, *Federalist Papers*, 6, 22.

78. James Madison, *Federalist Papers*, 10, 49: "Democracies have ever been the spectacle of turbulence and contention; have ever been found incompatible with personal security or the rights of property; and have in general been as short in their lives as they have been violent in their deaths."

79. Adams wondered: "What would Aristotle and Plato have said, if anyone had talked to them, of a federative republic of thirteen states, inhabiting a country of five hundred leagues in extent?" McCullough, *John Adams*, 397.

80. James Madison, *Federalist Papers*, 14, 72.

81. John Adams, letter to William Hooper, in McCullough, *John Adams*, 102.

82. McCullough, *John Adams*, 421–22.

Acknowledgments

Every book has a story, and the better the book the more people its story involves. If this book has any merit it is due to all of the people involved in it. To them go my thanks, all of my thanks, and my apologies if the book is not everything that it could be. I am grateful to Gwendolin Herder, my publisher, for all of our encouraging conversations about America. I am grateful to Roy M. Carlisle, my editor, for our delightful Friday conversations and for calling even when we did not have the book to discuss. My gratitude goes to Jean Blomquist for her careful editing and thoughts. I also need to thank Seana Sugrue, not just for accepting to write the foreword to this book, but for her meticulous reading of the manuscript and for pushing me to strengthen my arguments. My thanks go to Antonia Arslan, who read every chapter as it was being written with the graciousness, humor, and sarcasm that make her the great literary critic that she is. A thanks must also go to Father Joseph Koterski for his keen questions and discussions, to my colleagues at the University of Saint Thomas, Sandra Menssen, Mary Lemmons, Leora Weitzman, John Kronen, and to the chair of my department, Gary Atkinson, for their input. I must also thank Debbie Shelito, the philosophy department administrator, for taking the time to read the first draft of this book and for helping me to solve those problems that creep up in university life.

This book would also not have been as fun as it was to write had my students not become as involved in it as they did. Thank you Aaron Clevinger, Jennifer "Betty" Bennett, Dominika Kuzlak, Rachael Enns, Katherine Ellerhof, Molly Andreason, Jake Smokovitz, Jim Hall, Evan Dumas, and you many, many others who put up with my American rantings and added your own. And then there are my family to thank, my friends Mary Ortiz, Tona Varela, Uxue Diaz, Marta Minuzzi-Ostuni, Giovanna Crestani-Morassutti, Luisa di San Bonifacio, Piersandro Vanzan, and countless others. My special thanks go to the drivers of Saint Paul's All City Cab and 63 bus for all of the wonderful talks we had about our country as I was zipping from one place to another.

About the Author

Siobhan Nash-Marshall (Ph.D., Fordham University, 1998, Ph.D., Università Cattolica di Milano, 1997) is an Assistant Professor of Philosophy at the University of Saint Thomas in Saint Paul, Minnesota. She specializes in metaphysics and epistemology, and has published in both areas: *La Ricettività dell'Intelletto* (Milan: Vitae Pensiero, 2002), *Participation and the Good: A Study in Boethian Metaphysics* (New York: Herder & Herder/Crossroad Publishing Company, 2000), *Persona ed Essere* (Milan: Guerini, 1999).

Dr. Nash-Marshall enjoys writing for its own sake, has lived in many nations, and is deeply involved with the problem of nationhood. These traits first came together in her book *Joan of Arc: A Spiritual Biography* (New York: Crossroad Publishing Company, 1999), in which she attempted to understand how God could send a saint to save a nation.